Amazing Cat
Facts and Trivia

Le Chat Noir (1896) by Théophile Steinlen

Amazing **Cat**
Facts and Trivia

An illustrated collection of pussycat tales and feline facts

Tammy Gagne

CHARTWELL
BOOKS, INC.

A QUARTO BOOK

Published in 2011 by
Chartwell Books, Inc.
A division of Book Sales, Inc.
276 Fifth Avenue Suite 206
New York, New York 10001
USA

Reprinted 2013

Copyright © 2011 Quarto Inc.

ISBN-13: 978-0-7858-2835-8
ISBN-10: 0-7858-2835-4

Conceived, designed,
and produced by
Quarto Publishing plc
The Old Brewery
6 Blundell Street
London N7 9BH

QUA: CATO

Editor & designer:
Michelle Pickering
Art director: Caroline Guest
Indexer: Dorothy Frame

Creative director: Moira Clinch
Publisher: Paul Carslake

Color separation by Modern Age
Repro House Ltd, Hong Kong
Printed by Midas Printing
International Ltd, China

Contents

The contents of this book are completely random, so that each time you open it, you will discover an amazing variety of facts and trivia about the feline world. If you wish to locate a particular category of information, however, this contents listing is organized into topics. There is also an index at the end of the book.

Introduction 8

INTRODUCTION

As anyone who has ever owned a cat knows, no other animal on the planet is quite like this amazing creature. From longhaired beauties like the often-pampered Persian to shorthaired sensations like the sleek Bombay (it looks just like a miniature panther), cats seem to bewitch us the moment we lay eyes on them. It is not just their looks that captivate us, though. They also reel us in with their adorable habits, like rubbing against us (why do they do that?) and purring when they are content.

For centuries, people have tried to capture the feline essence in literature, song, and even superstition. Even longer ago, these curious companions were deified by the ancient Egyptians and immortalized in their carvings and other artifacts. Still, no one has been able to pinpoint exactly what makes a cat so catlike. Is it the animal's impressive talent for always landing on its feet (how exactly does it do that, anyway?) or is it the species' remarkable hunting prowess? While all of these things are part of what makes a cat what it is, no single attribute is the reason we adore our feline companions like we do.

Of course, cats also have their critics—people who insist on using words like sly and sneaky to describe this species' clever ways. More than one book or movie has stereotyped the cat as the scheming villain (*Lady and the Tramp*, anyone?). Other non-cat people may see the species as prissy—after all, no respectable cat enjoys being dirty, which is why cats spend so much time grooming themselves every day, but isn't this better than an animal that enjoys rolling in, well, things that your cat would prefer not to think about?

Cat fanciers know that the domesticated feline's fondness for good hygiene is one of the things that make it such an ideal pet. Show me a dog that arrives home essentially housetrained. (Do mother cats teach their kittens to use a litter box?) Cats also don't need our attention every waking moment the way many dogs do. Cats enjoy being with us, but they can tolerate our absence for brief periods of time without howling like there is no tomorrow.

If you love a cat, you know that doing so means giving it attention when it wants it—and giving it some space when it has had enough. (Kisses and hugs can be so yesterday!) Cat owners appreciate their pets for all that they are—playful, mysterious, soothing, comical, intelligent, athletic, and so much more. Most of all, we love our feline family members for the many ways in which they surprise us by adding to this list of qualities on a daily basis. So how does one define a cat? Only a cat can tell you for sure, but it probably won't.

My human feeds me, strokes me, plays with me, and loves me—it's so nice having a pet.

The Better to Sense You With

Cats have highly developed senses. As hunters, cats rely on their senses to locate prey, and depend on their sensory input in order to make a kill.

A cat's pupils are able to expand widely, giving excellent vision in very dim light conditions.

❶ **Sight:** A cat's eyes can detect the smallest of movements, even in extremely low light. It is a myth that cats can see in total darkness, but they can distinguish images in as little as one-fifth the amount of light that people and most animals need for seeing. This visual acuity gives wild cats a clear advantage against their prey when hunting at night.

❷ **Taste:** A cat's least acute sense is taste. Whereas people have about 10,000 taste buds on their tongues, cats have less than 500. This shortcoming does not mean that a cat does not enjoy eating, but it probably does mean that the cat takes more pleasure in the smell of food than in the taste.

❸ **Smell:** A cat may have a tiny nose, but its sense of smell is about 40 times more powerful than that of a human. A cat's nose contains as many as 200 million scent receptors. These cells alert the cat to the presence of other animals, even when they are in a different room or outdoors. A cat uses both its mouth and nose for smelling. Cats have a special organ in the roof of their mouth, called the vomeronasal organ, better known as the Jacobson's organ. A cat uses this organ to breathe in scents through its mouth; this is known as the flehmen reaction or flehming. When flehming, a cat may be so affected by a smell that it also starts to salivate.

A cat exhibiting the flehmen reaction stretches its neck, opens its mouth, and curls back its upper lip in a snarl.

❹ Hearing: Cats have acute hearing. Not only can a cat hear a sound from a considerable distance, but it can also discern the direction from which the noise came. A cat's hearing is a large part of what makes the species such adept mousers. While people cannot perceive the ultrasonic sounds made by small rodents, a cat's ears can identify sounds emitted at 60 to 65 kilohertz.

A cat's senses are on full alert as it hunts for prey.

❺ Touch: A domestic cat's most important sense is touch. A cat's fur is extremely sensitive to air movement, but its whiskers are even more perceptive. Located on the cheeks, lips, above the eyebrows, and on the back of the front legs, a cat's whiskers are in constant communication with a number of nerves. This highly tuned tactile network enables the animal to detect anything the whiskers touch. When navigating narrow spaces, a cat relies on its whiskers to judge the width. Interestingly, when a cat carries a mouse, it wraps its whiskers around it.

As Your Kitten Grows

By this age:	A kitten will:
10 days	Open its eyes and ears.
20 days	Crawl or stand.
4 weeks	Begin eating solid food.
	Cut its first teeth.
6 weeks	Begin to wean.
8 weeks	Groom itself.
3 months	Be ready to leave its mother.
	Reach its most playful phase.
	Understand the word "No."
4 to 6 months	Lose its baby teeth.
	Be old enough for flea preventative.
	Be ready for spaying or neutering.
9 to 12 months	Reach adolescence.
	Have developed its personality.
	Have nearly reached its full size.
18 months to 2 years	Reach physical and mental maturity.
	Become more interested in you.
	Be calmer.

THEY GROW OVERNIGHT! When kittens sleep, their bodies release an important growth hormone called dehydroepiandrosterone (DHEA).

Kittens are born blind and deaf, but have a strong sense of smell and a strong sucking reflex.

October

29

National Cat Day

In 2005, an animal welfare advocate named Colleen Paige declared October 29th to be National Cat Day. Paige's goal in creating this annual celebration of all things feline was to draw attention to the large number of cats in need of homes each year.

SOCIAL BUTTERFLIES

Some breeds are quicker than others to welcome new cats into their households. If you plan to get a second cat in the future, consider one of these breeds for your first feline pet:

✤ Birman
✤ British Shorthair
✤ Maine Coon
✤ Persian

Raccoon—no relation to the Maine Coon cat.

MAINE COON

The Maine Coon was the first longhaired cat to emerge naturally in North America. It gets its name from the US state of Maine, where it is believed to have originated, and the wild animal that the breed's coat resembles. (Don't believe the folklore that the breed is a cross between a domestic cat and a raccoon—such merging of species is biologically impossible.) This is a sizable cat, with males weighing as much as 18 pounds (8 kg) or more. Maine Coons are also known for their dense coats that add to the breed's overall hardiness. The breed includes more than 60 color and pattern combinations.

BEST IN SHOW

A tabby Maine Coon is recorded as having won the Best in Show award at the Madison Square Garden Cat Show in New York in 1895, the first benched cat show in the United States.

The Rough Side of the Tongue

A cat's tongue contains numerous backward-pointing hooks that help with self-grooming. These tiny barbs are also what make a cat's tongue feel like sandpaper when it licks you.

WHY DO CATS SPEND SO MUCH TIME GROOMING THEMSELVES?

Cats are painstakingly clean animals, and may spend as many as two or three hours each day grooming themselves. Although this may seem rather obsessive to humans, regular self-grooming is actually quite normal for this species.

✳ Cleanliness is only one reason that cats are so preoccupied with primping. They also groom themselves as a means of keeping warm during colder months. Licking smooths the fur, which traps warm air close to the animal's body. Licking also stimulates glands in the cat's skin that release secretions to help keep the coat resistant to water, which is especially important for an outdoor cat.

✳ You may notice that a cat begins cleaning itself immediately after you handle it. The cat is simply ridding itself of your scent and replenishing its own. A cat may also use grooming as a self-soothing measure when it feels stressed, not unlike the way a person might take a hot shower after a long, hard day.

✳ The only spots on a cat's body that its tongue cannot reach are its face, ears, and the back of its head. It is especially cute to watch a cat lick its front paws and then use them as a washcloth on these areas.

✳ If a cat is not grooming itself as thoroughly as usual, this may be a sign of illness. Excessive self-grooming can also be a sign of a behavioral or health problem—and can lead to bald patches or inflammation. If you have a longhaired cat, be sure to do your part by brushing it regularly to prevent mats and tangles. Some purebred cats even need an occasional bath to help keep them clean.

Sir Isaac Newton, discoverer of gravity—and inventor of the cat flap.

There's got to be an easier way to get inside than this!

ASTRONOMER, PHYSICIST, CAT OWNER...

Scientist Sir Isaac Newton (1643–1727) is credited with inventing the cat door. The story goes that Newton wanted his cats to have access to every room, including the dark room that he used for optical experiments. Newton cut a hole that his cat could pass through, and a smaller, lower hole for her kittens. He hung a black cloth over the openings to keep the light out, thereby inventing the first cat flap or cat door.

A Siamese cat nursing her kittens.

Nesting Behavior

When an expectant feline mother is in her final weeks of pregnancy, she will seek out potential sites for giving birth. She may root around in closets or cupboards and even appear to be cleaning house—preparing soft materials such as blankets or pillows by kneading them. She will continue to search and try out new places until she finds the one that she deems just right. When labor begins, she will return to this chosen spot to deliver her kittens.

The Evolution of the Cat

Fossilized remains indicate that the ancestors of today's cats appeared at about the same time as the dinosaurs became extinct, more than 60 million years ago.

❶ Miacis: This tree-climbing, weasel-like creature lived around 60 million years ago. It is thought to have been the common ancestor of all the carnivorous mammals that exist today, including both cats and dogs.

❷ Dinictis: It took another 10 million years for the first catlike carnivore to appear. Dinictis was about the same size as a lynx and looked very much like a modern cat, but its canine teeth were larger and its brain considerably smaller.

❸ Pseudaelurus: Appearing about 25 million years ago, Pseudaelurus, meaning "false cat," had the teeth of a true cat and almost walked on the tips of its toes, as all cats do.

❹ Felidae: The first true cats, Felidae, appeared about 12 million years ago. Most of the early felids have long since become extinct, such as Martelli's wildcat (*Felis lunensis*), but many have evolved further into the cats—both wild and domestic—that still survive and thrive.

Domestic cat

African wildcat

❺ Domestic cat: Genetic studies have revealed that the domestic cat (*Felis catus*) and the African wildcat (*Felis sylvestris lybica*) share the same genetic ancestor, with the progenitors of the domestic cat splitting from their wild relatives more than 100,000 years ago.

Comfortable

Pleased

Happy

Relaxed

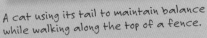

A cat using its tail to maintain balance while walking along the top of a fence.

DUAL PURPOSE

A cat uses its tail to express various types of emotion. For example, if the cat holds its tail upright and still when greeting you, this means that it is pleased to see you, and that it is feeling relaxed and comfortable. While the cat is being patted, its tail will quiver as a sign of pleasure. A wagging tail may indicate anger, but it can also be a sign that the cat is facing a dilemma—for instance, should it take the food being offered by a stranger or not? The tail also serves as an important tool for maintaining balance.

WHY DO CATS SMELL
OTHER CATS' URINE?

* When a female cat smells a male cat's urine, she learns a lot about him. For instance, she can tell how much fresh meat he has eaten recently. This information tells her whether he is a good hunter, and consequently helps her to determine if he is a suitable mate.

* When a male cat sniffs a female cat's urine, he can tell if she is in heat. A female cat will actually lift her tail and spray urine on objects to let her potential suitors know that she is available.

* The scent of urine can also tell a male cat whether the surroundings have been claimed by another male.

A Bengal cat smelling scent marks left by another feline.

A tabby cat beginning its cautious descent from a tall tree.

A LONG WAY DOWN

Cats are adept climbers, using their sharp claws and powerful hind legs to propel themselves upward. It is only when at the top of a tree that the cat's natural fear of heights comes flooding back, which can freeze the cat into immobility. The inward-curving claws do not help the cat if it tries to descend head first, and the cat will have to support its weight on its less powerful front legs. Many cats will jump from a low branch instead of trying to climb down the trunk, or else shimmy down backward. Whatever technique a cat uses, the overwhelming majority of cats will eventually come down—although the process may take hours.

Getting Your Cat Unstuck

For a species known for being such adept climbers, cats seem unlikely victims of getting trapped in trees. Still, some cats do indeed find themselves in this scary predicament.

* If your pet ever gets stuck, try to remain calm. If the cat is injured or has a leash wrapped around its neck, contact the local humane society at once. If there is no imminent danger, give the situation some time before taking action.

* Most cats eventually come down without assistance, but if yours does not, keep things low key. A swarm of onlookers will only make the cat more hesitant to descend. Instead, set out some of the cat's favorite food on the ground. Many cats have strong instinctual responses to the mealtime ritual. The cat may rush down to eat its dinner before it even realizes that it has done so. Be sure to choose something that your pet truly loves. For some cats, this may simply be a can of wet food; for others, it may be a can of sardines.

* If food does not do the trick, position a ladder against the tree. Be vigilant of any power lines that could come into contact with the ladder. Although you may be tempted to climb up to rescue your pet, give the cat a chance to come down on its own first. (Yes, a cat can indeed walk down a ladder.)

* If this strategy does not work and you decide to climb up to retrieve your pet, take all necessary precautions for your own safety—falls from ladders can cause serious injury and even death. Also bear in mind that the cat is probably feeling extremely anxious, so donning a jacket and a pair of thick gloves will protect you from getting scratched. Under no circumstances should you lean out and put yourself in danger in order to grab the cat.

* If your rescue efforts prompt the cat to climb even higher up the tree— or if the cat remains in the tree for more than 24 hours—contact the local humane society, which can advise you on who to call for help in your area. Fire departments will not always rush to the aid of cats stuck in trees like we see in the movies. Cost and liability may be cited as concerns, but you will not know the area's policy unless you make the call. Whichever organization does end up providing you with assistance, a donation may be a wonderful way of saying thank you.

"Cat"-astrophe?

Treats That Most Cats Love

❖ *Chicken*

❖ *Meat-based baby food*

❖ *Sardines*

❖ *Small pieces of cheese*

❖ *Tuna (but only serve occasionally because tuna contains a high amount of mercury)*

Egyptian Goddess

★ The Egyptian goddess Bastet was usually depicted as a seated cat or as a woman with the head of a cat or lion.

★ Bastet was a goddess of love and fertility, and the cat was connected with her because of the animal's natural fecundity. She was often depicted surrounded by kittens, or carrying a basket full of them.

★ Bastet was also a moon goddess. The pupils of a cat's eyes were thought to enlarge and contract with the waxing and waning of the moon.

★ The Egyptians considered that the cat's unblinking gaze gave it powers to seek out truth and to see the afterlife. Bastet was sometimes called the lady of truth, and was used in mummification ceremonies to ensure life after death.

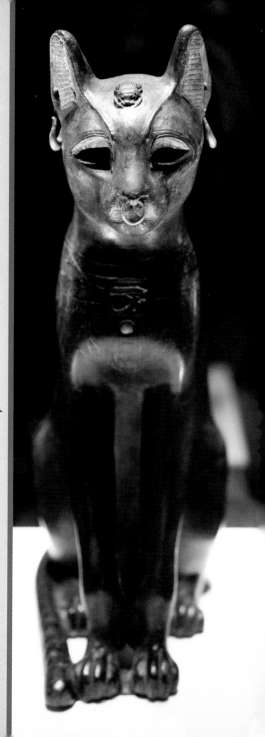

A seated bronze cat representing the goddess Bastet, found in Saqqara in Egypt and dating from the Late Period (after 600 B.C.E.).

Bastet as a cat-headed woman.

WITH ALL DUE RESPECT

Cats were held in such high regard in ancient Egypt that they ultimately achieved divine status and were treated with enormous respect.

✦ In ancient Egypt, the crime of killing a cat was punishable by death.

✦ Ancient Egyptians shaved their eyebrows as a sign of mourning when one of their cats died.

✦ In the 5th century B.C.E. when Persian soldiers attacked the Egyptian city of Pelusium, the soldiers positioned at the front line carried live cats as they marched toward the city walls. Just as the Persians predicted, the Egyptians chose to surrender instead of risking the lives of the revered felines.

As a sign of respect for the species, ancient Egyptian artists always depicted cats either hunting or seated in an upright position, never sleeping.

Pet Name
The first known cat to be given a name was Bouhaki, who appears in Egyptian carvings from as early as 1950 B.C.E.

The Egyptian Mau is a spotted cat, very similar to those pictured in ancient Egyptian scrolls and cartoons.

As Old as the Pyramids
The Egyptian Mau is one of the oldest cat breeds. The word "mau" was the ancient Egyptian word for cat, and also meant "to see" or "to foretell."

You Know That Saying About Curiosity…

It is not just a cliché—cats are indeed extremely curious creatures. Whether you are bringing a cat home for the first time or you have moved recently, your pet will want to explore virtually every inch of the new space. Don't let the cat's inquisitiveness get in the way of its safety.

A WARNING TO BE CAUTIOUS

The saying "Care [worry] kills a cat" first appeared in 1598 in the play Every Man in His Humour *by Ben Jonson. It evolved over time into "Curiosity killed the cat," sometimes with the addition of "but satisfaction brought it back."*

❖ **Close doors and windows where the cat should not have access.** Keep all windows and outside doors closed at all times if you do not want the cat to go outdoors. If you do not want the cat to explore cabinets and closets, be sure to close those doors, too. If they are lightweight and open easily, though, do not be surprised if your pet learns how to open them. Some cat owners have to use child safety equipment to keep their cats out of certain areas.

✤ Watch out for water.

Make sure that all fish tanks, rainwater storage tanks, hot tubs, and swimming pools are properly covered. Although cats can swim, they may panic if they fall into one of these basins unexpectedly. Also, close the door when you take a bath. If your pet falls into the tub, you will both be mighty unhappy about it. Many cats detest getting wet, and you could end up badly scratched.

✤ Watch out for fire.

Cover all fireplaces if not in use. You may be able to teach the cat that this area is off limits eventually, but it will likely take both time and effort. If you do use the fireplace, place a sturdy guard in front of it to keep your pet from burning itself. Also take care with cooking equipment, such as barbecues, where the smell of food may tempt the cat to investigate.

✤ Block off openings where the cat could hide or get trapped.

If you are remodeling, be especially careful of openings in walls or floors. Cats can hide in surprisingly small spaces. Some have even been trapped inside walls or under floorboards while renovations have taken place. Sharp edges, exposed nails, and tools can also be hazardous to your pet.

Are Cats Really Finicky Eaters?

Although they have a reputation for being picky eaters, most cats enjoy food. Some come running as soon as they hear the sound of a can opening or dry food being poured into a dish. If a cat suddenly stops eating, you can be sure there is a reason.

☆ **Is the food fresh?** Cats have an acute sense of smell. They know in a second if the food in front of them has been sitting in the refrigerator a little too long. Be sure to toss any leftover wet food within a few days.

☆ **Is the food a different consistency from what the cat normally eats?** Many cats have specific preferences when it comes to eating wet or dry food. Some will devour a flaked wet food formula, but turn their noses up at the same variety in the form of a paté.

☆ **Is the food warm enough?** If the cat cleaned its plate when you opened that new can of food last night but will not touch it today, it is probably a temperature issue. Certainly, you need to refrigerate leftover wet food once the container has been opened, but you should never serve it straight out of the fridge. A few seconds in the microwave might be all you need to do to make the cat gobble down leftovers as voraciously as the first serving.

☆ **Does the food contain a new ingredient?** Even if you buy the same brand of food, the cat may not appreciate your attempt at offering it variety by going with the salmon instead of the chicken or turkey that it is accustomed to eating. Most cats have one or two favorite foods. If you decide to try something new, purchase only a small quantity of the new formula until you are sure that the cat will eat it.

☆ **Have you changed the location of the cat's dishes?** Most cats prefer to dine in a quiet corner of a room instead of in the middle of the household hustle and bustle. If even the corner of the room seems boisterous, consider moving the cat's dishes to another room where privacy is a bit more plentiful.

Excuse me, this isn't what I ordered.

WHEN TO GO TO THE VET

Keep an eye on the cat to make sure that it is eating something. If your pet does not consume any food for more than 48 hours, it may be suffering from a health issue and should see a vet as soon as possible.

How Do Cats Find Their Way Home?

Many animals can find their way home after being released, either intentionally or accidentally. Scientists refer to this ability as homing—think homing pigeons. Cats, too, possess this useful trait, and there are astonishing stories of cats traveling over a thousand miles to return to their old home after a house move. This homing ability is thought to be linked to a magnetic structure in the animal's brain that acts as an internal compass of sorts.

IF YOUR CAT IS MISSING

1) *Search your home thoroughly. Check inside closets and cupboards, behind doors, and underneath furniture. Remember that cats love to hide in small spaces.*

2) *Once you are certain that the cat is not inside, check outside. Check the garage, shed, and yard completely. When it is cold or wet outdoors, some cats will seek shelter underneath automobiles.*

3) *Ask family members and friends to help you search for the cat while you post flyers around the neighborhood offering a reward for your pet's return. Be sure to include the cat's name, a recent photograph (preferably in color), and your contact information. List a physical description, noting any distinguishing marks. Ask local businesses if you may place flyers in their windows or on their bulletin boards. Be on the lookout for your pet as you post these notices.*

4) *Visit your local animal shelter and veterinarian's office. If there is an animal emergency hospital nearby, check there as well. Ask if an animal matching the cat's description has been brought in—and if not, to contact you immediately if one does appear. Post flyers before leaving these establishments.*

CAN I COOK FOR MY CAT?

Cats require a specific list of nutrients. Moreover, they must be delivered in precise amounts and in the right ratio in order for your pet to reap their benefits. Occasionally, a vet may recommend that owners of sick cats cook for their pets, but in general, owners' time is better spent carefully selecting a high-quality prepackaged diet.

A cat requires lots of protein in its diet.

Fostering

Animal shelters utilize volunteers who are willing to provide temporary homes for cats with special needs. Many female cats that end up in shelters are pregnant. Ideally, these cats should be able to give birth and wean their kittens in a home environment, because they will be exposed to far less stress and fewer illnesses this way. Once the kittens are ready to be adopted, the mother cats can be spayed and placed in permanent homes themselves. By providing foster care, you can make a real difference in the life of an animal. Fostering is also a great way to build your cat care knowledge and experience.

kittens get a much better start in life if they are born and cared for in a loving home.

RAINING CATS AND DOGS

For years, an email has been circulating that states the supposed origin of this phrase. In the often forwarded message about life in the 1500s, the recipients are told that pets settled into the straw in thatched roofs to stay warm. Such accommodations would become slippery when wet, so the email states that when animals slipped and fell from the thatch, people would say, "It's raining cats and dogs!" The even sadder yet more likely origin is found in Jonathan Swift's 1710 poem, "A Description of a City Shower." During this period in history, heavy rain would collect in the streets and carry dead animals and other debris from one location to another.

Did You Know?

A group of kittens is called a kindle. A group of cats is called a clowder.

A kindle of kittens.

ANNE FRANK

Anne Frank, the teenage Jewish girl known for the diary she kept while in hiding from the Nazis during World War II, loved cats. She owned several during her short lifetime, and mentioned four by name in her diary.

★ **Moortje**, her own black cat that she had to leave behind with neighbors when her family went into hiding.

★ **Mouschi**, the cat of another family who joined the Franks in hiding.

★ **Moffie** (sometimes translated as Boche), a warehouse cat living in the building where the family hid.

★ **Tommy**, another warehouse cat that used to fight with Moffie and had run away by the time Anne began her diary.

DO CATS DREAM?

No one knows for certain whether cats dream when they sleep, but many owners regularly observe signs of dreaming in their pets. A sleeping cat may move its paws, flick its ears, or twitch its whiskers. Some cats even make noises in their sleep, indicating that something is going on behind those closed eyes.

ON SLEEPING

"Kittens are born with their eyes shut. They open them in about six days, take a look around, then close them again for the better part of their lives." Stephen Baker

zzzZZZZZ...

CATNAPPING

A healthy adult cat can sleep for up to 16 hours a day. This means that a three-year-old cat has been awake for only about one year of its life.

Playtime

Never underestimate the value of playtime. Play is good for a cat's physical and mental health, and it can be pretty fun for you, too. Strive to spend about 15 minutes twice a day playing with your cat. In addition to providing exercise and stimulation, you will be deepening the bond between you and your pet.

Cat Toys: The most obvious way to play with a cat are with its toys. Balls that light up or spin around tracks, catnip mice, and fishing poles with tantalizing feathers on the end can all capture the cat's attention.

Impromptu Toys: If no cat toys are available, improvise. A ping pong ball, a piece of string—even a cardboard tube with an edible treat inside can be entertaining. Household objects, like ribbon and even crumpled paper, also make great impromptu cat toys. A small ball of yarn is not enough to knit anything, but it can provide a cat with hours of enjoyment.

Hours of fun with just a piece of string.

Paper Bags: Most cats love to play with paper bags. Just leave one open on the floor and the cat will do the rest. To make it even more fun, gently tap the bag from the outside once the cat enters it. Your pet will likely bat at your hand, trying to catch it.

Warning: Paper Only

Only paper bags should be used as toys for cats. Never give a plastic bag to a cat due to the risk of suffocation that they pose.

Flashlights and Laser Pointers: A dark room and a flashlight can provide lots of fun for a cat. Just shine the light around the room, and watch your feline companion chase the elusive beam. You can also find laser pointers made for this purpose at pet supply stores.

Laser pointer keyring

Peekaboo: Playful kittens love to play peekaboo. Begin by moving slowly and using a whispery voice so that you do not frighten your young cat. As the kitten gets older, this game can evolve into hide and seek. Most cats love to play hunter, stalking their prey before pouncing on it like a fearless lion or tiger.

Cat and Mouse Games: Using a blanket or a sheet of newspaper, play a game of cat and mouse with your pet. You be the mouse by reaching underneath the covering with your hand. The cat will be delighted to chase the elusive prey by pouncing on top of it. The longer you can keep the cat from catching you, the longer the game will be.

Bubbles: Many cats enjoy chasing soap bubbles blown by their owners.

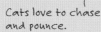

Cats love to chase and pounce.

Tiger tabby a.k.a. mackerel tabby a.k.a. striped tabby.

What do you mean I can't roar?! Grrrr, prrrr, purrrr,... Oops!

The Cat Family

Cats have evolved on all continents except Australia and Antarctica. The domestic cat is one of about 40 different species of cat that exist today. These 40 species can be divided into two groups:

✢ **Panthera:** This group includes the big cats that can roar, such as lions and tigers. They have a small hyoid bone at the base of their tongue that moves about freely, which enables them to roar.

✢ **Felinae:** This group includes the smaller cats that cannot roar, such as bobcats, lynx, and domestic cats. They have a rigid hyoid bone, which means that they cannot roar.

TIGER TABBIES

❋ *The most common tabby pattern is the striped tabby.*

❋ *Striped tabbies are sometimes called tiger tabbies, because of the resemblance to a tiger's stripes.*

❋ *They are also known as mackerel tabbies, because the pattern looks like the bones of a fish.*

Vietnamese years of the cat.

ZODIAC CAT

☆ In Chinese astrology, there are 12 animal signs in the zodiac. Each animal governs a year, with the 12 animals rotating in a regular annual cycle.

☆ One of the 12 animals is the tiger. Tiger people are said to be daring and passionate.

☆ Another animal in the Chinese zodiac is the rabbit, but in Vietnamese astrology, the rabbit is replaced by the cat. Cat/rabbit people are intuitive and sensitive.

An adolescent Siberian tiger. Adults can weigh up to 700 pounds (320 kg).

LARGER MEMBERS
OF THE CAT FAMILY

- Cheetah
- Jaguar
- Leopard
- Lion
- Lynx
- Ocelot
- Panther
- Puma
- Serval
- Tiger

TIGER, TIGER, BURNING BRIGHT
The largest of all non-hybrid cat species is the tiger, and the largest of these is the Siberian tiger. The stripes on a tiger's body provide good camouflage, serving to break up the tiger's outline, particularly in the heavily forested areas that form the animal's natural habitat. Each tiger has a unique pattern of stripes.

Selecting a Healthy Cat

You cannot tell if an animal is completely healthy just by looking at it, but a quick inspection can tell you many things about a cat's general well-being.

❶ **Look into the cat's eyes.** They should be wide open and clean, with no cloudiness, redness, or discharge. The third eyelid should not be visible.

❷ **Check the cat's ears.** They should be clean, with no discharge or redness. Incessant itching could be a sign of fleas or mites. Ear infections are rare in cats, but they do occur. If you notice a foul odor in the ear, an infection is the most likely problem.

❸ **Touch the cat's nose.** It should feel cool and slightly wet. Any discharge or crustiness could indicate an upper respiratory infection (URI). Repeated sneezing is also a sign of a URI.

❹ **Gently open the cat's mouth.** Its gums should be light pink, with no swelling, redness, or bleeding. Bad breath could be a sign of a health problem.

❺ **Run your hand over the cat.** The fur should feel smooth and look glossy. An extremely dry coat could indicate a skin problem. You are not likely to see a flea even if the cat is suffering from an infestation, but prolonged scratching should be a red flag. You can identify a flea problem by rubbing a comb through the cat's fur and then wiping it with a white towel. Black or red specks are signs of a flea problem.

❻ **Check the cat's abdomen.** It should be reasonably round but not overly so. Pot-bellied cats often have roundworms.

A healthy cat's fur will look glossy and feel smooth.

BRITISH INVASION

British Shorthairs are known for their intelligence and their agreeable temperaments. These cats are often cast in movies and television commercials because they can be trained so easily.

Playing It By Ear

Have you ever noticed that cats often move their ears when they hear a particular sound? They do this to pinpoint the exact location of the noise. A cat has more than 20 muscles in each of its ears that make these tiny movements possible.

Third Eyelid

Cats have a third eyelid called the palpebra tertia or nictitating membrane. Cats have especially large corneas, and this inner membrane serves as extra protection against injuries.

Third eyelid

ON AND OFF

Female cats are polyestrous, which means that they go into heat multiple times each year. An unspayed female can become fertile every two or three weeks between early spring and late fall unless she becomes pregnant or is spayed by a veterinarian.

REASONS A SHELTER
MAY TURN YOU DOWN

Animal shelters assess potential cat owners to make sure that their cats go to suitable homes. If a shelter turns you down, it may be because:

✦ You are not the right match for the cat you want to adopt.

✦ You have other animals that are unlikely to be a good match for the cat.

✦ You have too many pets.

✦ You have young children.

✦ You travel too much.

✦ You plan to allow the cat to roam freely outdoors (many shelters in the United States, for example, prefer a cat to be kept indoors because of environmental dangers) or you plan to keep the cat indoors (in countries like Britain, some shelters prefer cats to have some form of outdoor access).

✦ You plan to declaw the cat (declawing is very controversial, and is illegal in some countries).

✦ You work too many hours.

Why can't I go home with you?

WHAT TO DO NEXT

If your adoption application is not approved, consider the reasons. If the problem is finding the right match, consider adopting a different cat. If having young children is the reason, perhaps apply again once the kids are a bit older. If a shelter insists that their cats be kept as indoor pets but you do not want a litter box, ask yourself whether this is truly a deal breaker. No matter what the reasons are, don't be too hard on yourself. Maybe you are just not ready to become a cat owner at this moment in your life. If you still want a cat, give yourself a little time. Your circumstances may be very different in just a few months or a year down the road.

Mind and Body

Kittens mature much faster physically than mentally. A cat may reach physical adulthood between the ages of 6 months and 1 year, but it may be another year before the cat behaves like an adult.

DOGLIKE CATS
The following breeds
are said to be doglike
in personality:

- American Curl
- Burmese
- Chartreux
- Cornish Rex
- Devon Rex
- Japanese Bobtail
- Maine Coon
- Manx
- Ocicat
- Scottish Fold
- Siberian
- Tonkinese
- Turkish Van

HOW TO TEACH A CAT TO PLAY FETCH

Cats do not learn tricks like dogs do, but you may be able to teach a cat to play fetch—provided you are patient. Begin by selecting the cat's favorite toy. Toss the object across the floor in front of the cat to encourage your pet to go after it. Let the cat play with the toy for a few seconds, then go and take the toy from the cat and return to your original position. Encourage the cat to follow you there and praise it when it does so. By repeating this over and over, the cat just might bring the item back to you so that you can toss it again. The best time to work on teaching fetch is right before the cat's dinner. Cats are typically most attentive just before meals.

The Purring Poodle

In addition to its canine nickname—the purring poodle—the Devon Rex is known for wagging its tail when happy.

Devon Rex

A Dog in a Cat's Coat

Owners report that the Ocicat enjoys playing fetch, learning commands, and walking on a leash.

The Ocicat is so-named because it looks like a baby ocelot.

NOT ENOUGH ROOM TO SWING A CAT

When people say that there is not enough room to swing a cat, they mean that the space is particularly small. Although this phrase certainly brings to mind a vivid image, it is doubtful that it refers to an actual animal. During the 17th century, knotted cords called cat o'nine tails were used as whips to punish sailors in the British Navy. The phrase likely refers to swinging one of these whipping devices.

FLEA AND TICK PREVENTATIVES

✳ Many cat owners use medicated collars to help keep fleas and ticks off their pets. However, the majority of flea collars are impregnated with chemicals and there is some concern that these can be toxic to anyone who touches them; indeed, some cats do have an allergic reaction to flea collars. In addition, a flea collar may not eradicate a flea problem on its own, so other methods of flea control would have to be used anyway.

✳ If you are concerned, ask a veterinarian about using a flea and tick preventive medication. Most of these products are used topically once a month. Once applied to the skin, the medication spreads over the cat's entire body over a 24- to 48-hour period. The active ingredients in this medication do not harm the cat or anyone it encounters—besides the fleas and ticks, of course.

Flea

Tick

No Substitutions!
Never use a flea treatment made for dogs on a cat. Even a small amount of a product made for dogs can make a cat sick, or even kill it.

Mite

MITES OR MANGE
If a cat is scratching its ears constantly, it could have ear mites, which can lead to the skin condition mange. If you suspect that the cat has mites, take it to the vet at once.

Does Heat Hurt?

No one knows for certain whether estrus is painful for female cats. However, most cats make yowling noises when they are in heat, so it is safe to assume that they feel at least a bit uncomfortable during this time.

A female cat displaying her readiness to mate by rubbing up against a male cat.

LONG-DISTANCE RELATIONSHIPS
When a male cat is looking for a mate, he may travel more than three times his typical distance from home.

CLOSE TO HOME

❖ When allowed to roam freely outdoors, an unneutered male cat's territory is usually significantly larger than that of a sterilized male or a female cat.

❖ Female cats tend to stay relatively close to home, but male suitors may come from miles around if they smell a female in heat.

❖ To prevent unwanted pregnancies in females and to reduce a male cat's chances of straying too far from home, have your cat spayed or neutered.

Litter Box Training

If your new cat has not already been trained to use a litter box, it will be your job to teach your pet. Cats are by nature clean and fastidious, so litter box training is usually not difficult.

❶ Place the litter box in a quiet, secluded corner where the cat will not be disturbed. Bathrooms and laundry rooms are often ideal spots, but a quiet corner in any room may work fine, too. Cats prefer not to eat in close proximity to where they eliminate, so situate the litter box far away from the cat's food dishes. If you do not take this simple step, the cat may let you know that it is displeased by eliminating in another part of the home instead.

❷ Make sure that there is enough litter in the box for the cat to scratch a hole and cover it over again— approximately ½–2 inches (13–50 mm) deep. Place the cat gently in the box, and let it get used to the smell and feel of the litter.

❸ Establish a routine of placing the cat gently in the box whenever it looks ready to use it. If training a kitten, always put it in the box after it has eaten, because eating prompts a kitten to eliminate almost immediately.

❹ At first, the cat may not know how to use the box, and it may soil elsewhere in the house. Don't shout at your pet, and never rub its nose in the mess—the smell will only encourage the cat to use this spot again. Simply say "No!" in a firm but quiet voice, and place the cat in the litter box.

❺ If a cat continually refuses to use the litter box, move it to another spot and try using a different litter. Alternatively, try a method such as containment training.

Don't forget to buy a scoop when purchasing a litter box.

TAKING COVER
Many cats prefer to eliminate in private, so it may be wise to invest in a litter box with a cover. Some models even include flap-style doors for added privacy.

A kitten being litter box trained using the containment method.

NO TWO ALIKE
A cat's nose has a unique pattern, just like a human being's fingerprint.

Look, I'm using the litter box. Can I come out now please?

CONTAINMENT TRAINING

One way of litter box training your pet is to contain the cat within a wire crate or pen with a cover.

❶ Place the pen in an area of the home that can be cleaned easily—on a tile floor, for example. Cover the entire floor of the cage with litter. The initial goal is to give the cat no other choice than to use the litter when it needs to eliminate. You must keep the cat in its crate continuously in order for this method to be successful.

❷ After a few days, remove all of the litter from the cage floor and clean the cage. Now provide the cat with a small litter box in one corner of the crate. Your pet should be trained to use the box within another few days.

❸ At this point, open the crate or remove it entirely. However, do not simply give the cat access to the entire home all at once. Instead, contain the cat to this one room until you are sure that it is fully trained.

KITTEN TRAINING

❂ A kitten is certainly old enough for litter box training as soon as it is old enough to go home with you—that is, 12 weeks of age—but some breeders start working on the task before this time.

❂ The sides of a kitten's litter box should be no more than 4 inches (10 cm) high. Once the kitten has reached its full size, you may want to invest in a box with higher sides to keep your pet from tossing litter onto the floor or carpeting.

Teach children to handle cats gently, and discourage them from trying to lift a cat unless you are present to supervise. Preschoolers should always be supervised.

Cats and Kids

Choosing to add a cat to your household can be a huge decision. If you have children, you probably have even more questions and concerns. Are the kids old enough for a cat? Can a cat hurt the children? How much time and care does a cat require? What if you are expecting a baby?

❂ The kids' ages are less important than your vigilance. Even if a child is very mature, young kids and pets must be supervised at all times. A child might inadvertently injure a cat by simply trying to play with it—and the cat may react by scratching. Lessons in correct handling and general respect for animals should be an ongoing part of family life with a cat.

❂ Older kids pose less concern of harming the cat accidentally, but you need to be watchful when new friends visit. Children who have never been around cats may not know how to treat them properly. Sadly, some kids will abuse animals if given the chance.

❂ Cats are relatively low-maintenance pets. Unless you select a longhaired breed, your pet will not need daily brushings. Since cats are such meticulous self-groomers, bathing is not usually necessary, regardless of hair length. Still, any pet needs regular attention and care. The cat must be given fresh food and water daily, and you will need to keep its litter box clean. An adolescent may be capable of performing these tasks, but it is important not to make a child the sole caregiver of an animal. Homework, extracurricular activities, and socializing can bump a pet down to the bottom of a teen's to-do list. Always check to make sure that the cat has not been forgotten.

❂ If you are just starting a family, it may be wise to wait before adding a new pet to the mix. In addition to being less stressful for you, waiting will help your future cat to see the infant as part of the household, not as an intruder that disrupts its routine.

❂ Some pregnant women are susceptible to an infection called toxoplasmosis. This microscopic parasite is shed through a cat's fecal matter and can cause birth defects if proper hygiene is not followed. If you already own a cat, you should wear gloves when handling the cat's litter box—or better yet, ask another family member to clean the box. You can also ask a doctor about a blood test to determine if you are immune to the infection; many people are.

SAFETY NETS

When cat owners become parents, they may worry that the cat will sneak into the baby's crib when the newborn is napping. They may even fear that the cat could smother the sleeping infant. The latter scenario is highly unlikely, but it is possible that a cat could inadvertently injure a baby by jumping into the crib or scratching at the bedding material. The best way to prevent unnecessary injury is by placing a net over the crib when the baby is sleeping. You can find this item at a store that sells baby supplies.

CELTIC CATS

The Book of Kells, an illuminated copy of the Gospels made in Ireland during the 8th century, contains many pictures of cats. They tend to represent judgment and are often depicted with mice or rats, which represent human souls.

A TRUE CINDERELLA STORY

Thailand was the setting for an extravagant cat wedding in 1996. The bride and groom were "diamond-eyed" cats, possessing a rare type of feline glaucoma believed to be a sign from God. Phet and Ploy arrived at the ceremony in a Rolls-Royce and a helicopter, respectively. The best man was a parrot, and the maid of honor was an iguana. The cats' owners spent the equivalent of $17,000 on the eccentric celebration, which more than 500 guests attended. The feline couple received more than $60,000 worth of gifts.

Best man

Maid of honor

Why would you want a piglet in the bag when you can have me?

TO LET THE CAT OUT OF THE BAG

Today, letting the cat out of the bag means divulging a secret. It is thought that at one time this phrase had both figurative and literal meaning. Shrewd customers who bought pigs at the market would check to make sure that the bags they received did indeed contain piglets. When a sneaky seller had substituted a cat in place of a piglet, the patron would let the cat out of the bag, exposing the merchant's scam.

The Indoor/Outdoor Debate

**Many owners keep their cats indoors because they believe
it to be safer. Others feel that it is more natural and
kinder to allow cats the freedom to roam outside.**

* Outdoor cats are more vulnerable to encounters with
automobiles and predators, and may be exposed to contagious
illnesses from other felines. Owners must be extra vigilant for
signs of ill-health—for example, it is easier to miss problems
such as persistent constipation or diarrhea that require
veterinary assistance. As skilled hunters, outdoor cats
may also have an impact on local wildlife numbers.

* Indoor cats can become bored, leading to stress, inactivity,
and obesity. An outdoor environment is full of stimulation.
It is crucial for owners of indoor cats to provide a stimulating
environment within the home in order to keep their pets both
mentally and physically active. Destructive scratching may also
be a problem for some owners.

Stimulate indoor cats with toys, and provide some
means for the cat to relieve its desire to scratch.

Outdoor cats get plenty
of stimulation from the
outdoor environment and
lots of opportunities to
strop their claws.

WHAT TYPE OF AGGRESSION IS THIS?

Match each description to one of the types of aggression.

Description

1) A cat that acts aggressively for no apparent reason, has always had a poor temperament in general, and may also fall short of its individual breed standard.

2) A cat that lives with a child that constantly teases it, and bullies other cats in its household.

3) A cat that normally behaves well but turns aggressive when frightened.

4) A friendly cat that becomes aggressive when other cats enter its home or yard.

5) A mild-mannered cat that gets overly excited when playing, sometimes to the point of acting aggressively.

6) An unneutered male cat that tries to kill kittens sired by another tom cat.

7) A male cat that gets into a fight with a female cat in heat.

8) A cat that stands guard over the food dishes of the other cats in its household.

9) A cat that hunts smaller animals like birds and rodents.

10) A mother cat that acts aggressively toward anyone who poses a threat to her kittens.

Type of Aggression

a) Fear aggression

b) Food aggression

c) Inbred aggression

d) Maternal aggression

e) Paternal aggression

f) Play aggression

g) Prey aggression

h) Redirected aggression

i) Sexual aggression

j) Territorial aggression

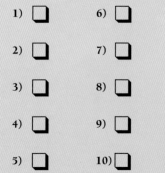

Play aggression between kittens.

1) ☐   6) ☐

2) ☐   7) ☐

3) ☐   8) ☐

4) ☐   9) ☐

5) ☐   10)☐

Answers: 1=c; 2=h; 3=a; 4=j; 5=f; 6=e; 7=i; 8=b; 9=g; 10=d

Kittens should stay with their mother until they are at least 12 weeks old.

Critical Age

⭑ Be leery of a breeder who allows customers to take kittens home before they are at least 12 weeks old. Staying with its mother and littermates for the first 12 weeks of its life is important for a kitten's healthy development. Leaving its mother any earlier could result in social, emotional, and health issues.

⭑ The early weeks of a kitten's life are a critical socialization period. If a kitten spends a good deal of time with people and has positive interactions with them during this time, it is much more likely to grow into a friendly, well-adjusted cat.

FACTORS THAT DETERMINE PERSONALITY

• Breed
• Gender
• Genetics
• Health
• History
• Socialization
• Sterilization

WHO'S YOUR DADDY?

Genes play an important role in the temperament of a cat. A friendly cat is more likely to produce friendly kittens. Interestingly, it is the genes that a kitten inherits from its father that have the biggest impact on how outgoing it will be. The mother's genes also play a part, as does the maternal nurturing process, but the father's genetic material has a greater influence than the mother's on a kitten's personality.

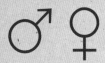

Sexing a Cat

To determine a cat's gender, gently lift its tail and inspect the area beneath it. If the two openings are close together, the cat is female. If they are farther apart, the cat is male.

Voyage to a New World

* *Christopher Columbus may have taken cats with him on his first voyage to America in 1492, but it is recorded that he certainly took them on his second visit in 1493–95.*

* *Documents show that several cats arrived with the Pilgrims on the Mayflower in 1620.*

IN AND OUT
Cats purr upon inhaling as well as exhaling.

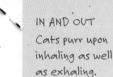

Christopher Columbus

500 de ani de la descoperirea Americii de către Cristofor Columb

POSTA ROMÂNA 6 L

WHY DO CATS PURR?

Purring is often a sign of happiness, but many cats also purr at times when they are anything but content. A cat may purr as a means of comforting itself when feeling stressed, or it may purr to let another cat know that it has no ill intentions. Interestingly, purring is a self-healing as well as self-soothing behavior. A cat's purring falls between 25 and 150 hertz. Scientists assert that sounds within this range actually speed the healing of bones, ligaments, muscles, and tendons. Perhaps this is why cats experience more rapid recoveries from broken bones than dogs do.

PURR...
Most kittens begin purring when they are about one week old.

CATS WITH DISABILITIES

If you are searching for a cat to adopt, please don't rule out an animal with a disability. Whether a cat has lost its eyesight, its hearing, or one of its legs, it can still make a wonderful pet for the right person. Animals are much more resilient than most people when it comes to this type of adversity. They are also surprisingly resourceful. Blind cats utilize their keen senses of smell and hearing, as well as their whiskers, to help them navigate. Deaf cats can be taught a variety of hand signals for owners to use in place of words and phrases. Amputees may look a little awkward at first, but they get by amazingly well on three paws.

A cat that loses a leg will quickly learn to get around on just three.

Feeling Things Out

A blind cat will sweep its head side to side while walking so that it can use its whiskers in a similar way to a blind person using a cane.

It's a Guy Thing

Just as a person has a dominant hand, a cat typically uses one front paw more than the other. This primary appendage has been associated with gender in both humans and felines. Most female cats are right-pawed, whereas males tend to be left-pawed. The numbers are a little different for people, but the trend is the same. Only about 10 percent of the human population is left-handed, but more often than not those lefties are male.

Left-pawed cats are usually male.

The Mongrels

* The overwhelming majority of the world's cat population falls into the category affectionately known as the alley cat or moggie—an all-sorts mongrel mixture of breeds, brought about by centuries of enthusiastic promiscuity. Mongrels are most often shorthaired, although no strict rules can ever apply, and they can be a walking riot of colors.

* While it is easier to predict what the temperament of pedigree cats is likely to be, mongrels are certainly not lacking in character. They can become just as devoted to their owners and are no more susceptible to illness than pedigree cats. Equal care should be taken when obtaining a non-pedigree cat from a friend or shelter.

Mongrel cats come in a multitude of colors.

LOOK BEFORE YOU DRIVE
If you have an outdoor cat or live in a neighborhood with cats that roam freely, always look under your vehicle before getting into it. Some cats use parked automobiles for shelter, not realizing how dangerous this habit is.

Mongrels—uniquely wonderful!

A dangerous place to shelter.

TRUE OR FALSE?
Cats have whiskers on their legs.

Answer: True. In addition to the whiskers on the faces, cats have small whiskers on the back of their front legs. These sensitive hairs are located behind the carpus, or wrist. Leg whiskers help a cat to determine the size and exact location of prey animals.

Whiskers on the front legs help a cat when hunting.

DO CATS GRIEVE?

Like people, cats are affected by the loss of loved ones. Cats grieve for their favorite humans, as well as fellow house pets, when these companions pass away. Also like people, cats sometimes have a hard time dealing with their loss. Here are some things that owners can do to help grieving pets:

❖ Give the cat something that belonged to the person or animal it is grieving. Ideally, this should be an item that your pet can cuddle up with, like a blanket, a piece of clothing, or a soft toy.

❖ Maintain the cat's routine. The cat has already experienced enough change. Getting up and going to bed at the same times each day, eating meals at the usual hours, and even keeping up with regular grooming is comforting to an animal that has lost a central figure in its life.

❖ Don't skip playtime. Even if the cat does not seem interested at first, keep trying to engage it. Exercise is essential for your pet's mental and physical health. When a cat is active, its body releases endorphins. These natural body chemicals literally make the cat feel better.

❖ Spend time with the cat. As simple as it sounds, just being with you is reassuring to your pet in times of trouble. Give the cat as much attention as possible, and ask any visitors to the home to do the same.

❖ Spoil your pet a little. Interactive toys are a great way to occupy a cat's time, especially when you cannot be with your pet. Feeding the cat meals made with its favorite ingredients is another way to indulge your pet.

Make a point of eating meals together to make the cat feel a little less alone, especially if it is grieving the loss of a fellow pet.

❖ Although you may be tempted to get another cat to keep your grieving pet company, this is a bad idea—at least for the time being. Once the cat is acting more like itself, you can consider offering it new feline companionship. Making this move too soon, however, could lead to the resident cat's rejection of the newcomer.

A grieving cat can find comfort by cuddling a blanket that belonged to the deceased.

REACHING OUT

If you are grieving the loss of a feline friend, you may feel very alone, but there are people who understand your situation. Reach out to them. An internet search for "pet loss support" will help you to find online and local pet bereavement support groups and agencies. There are also books available with practical advice for grieving owners.

A Bengal and Maine Coon sitting on a window perch and watching the world go by.

A ROOM WITH A VIEW

Many cats enjoy being able to look out of the window and watch what is going on outside.

◆ A window perch is a great idea if the window sills in your home are not wide enough to accommodate a cat. Resembling a shelf, this padded item affords the cat with a comfy place to sit or lie while taking in some outdoor scenery. Most perches are extremely easy to set up. Some models are freestanding and may even include a scratching post.

◆ When placing a cat's window perch, consider the location carefully. If you have a tree in the yard that attracts birds and squirrels—and the cat likes to watch wildlife— a window on that side of the home will make the best seat in the house for your pet. Some cats enjoy sitting where they can watch traffic go by their homes. Others prefer a quiet spot that gets plenty of warm sun. If you find the cat on its window perch regularly, chances are good that you have chosen the perfect spot for it.

IF YOU LIKE THE LOOK OF BIG CATS

A few breeds of domestic cat bear a striking resemblance to their larger wild relatives. These include:

- American Bobtail
- Bengal
- Ocicat
- Savannah
- Sokoke
- Toyger

How much??!!!!

MOST EXPENSIVE CAT

Until 1998, the record for the most expensive cat ever sold was held by a California Spangled. It was bought in the United States for $24,000 in 1987, and had appeared in the Neiman Marcus department store's Christmas catalog the previous year. The record was broken when a Bengal was bought in England for £25,000 (around $41,000).

The Bengal is like a miniature leopard with a loving nature. It has a cooing or chirruping call that adds to the impression that it is a wild cat.

Controversial Cat

The California Spangled may be a rare breed, but many people know about it. Paul Arnold Casey saw to that. A Hollywood writer, Casey developed the breed in the 1980s to look like a wild leopard, although it has no wild blood. The controversy began when Casey decided to advertise his cats in the 1986 Neiman Marcus Christmas catalog as "his and hers" gifts for $1,400 each. It was not the high price that cat lovers took issue with, but rather what they saw as complete disrespect for these cats by marketing them like designer handbags or jewelry.

Grooming Your Cat

Most cats benefit from grooming, and longhaired breeds such as the Persian must be groomed daily to keep the full coat in good condition and to prevent the soft undercoat from matting. Shorthaired cats require less grooming than longhairs, but a regular brushing will help to keep the cat's coat clean and shiny. The grooming routine does not need to be complicated, and tools to simplify the process are readily available from pet stupply stores.

REASONS FOR GROOMING

★ Not only does grooming make a cat look good, but it also makes the cat feel good. A dirty or matted coat is uncomfortable for a cat. Grooming spreads the essential oils released by the cat's skin throughout its coat.

★ Grooming also allows you to give your pet a health check. During a grooming session, you can identify and remove fleas, and even more importantly, check your pet for any worrisome changes. Bald patches, cuts, or skin growths can indicate serious health problems, but a vet will have a much better chance of treating any illness successfully if you catch it early.

I'm really not sure whether I like this...

GET AN EARLY START

Get a kitten used to being groomed at a young age. In the beginning, brush your pet's coat at least once a day, even if it is a shorthaired cat. Trim claws whenever necessary. Touch the kitten's paws often, so that your pet gets used to having its feet handled. You may even want to give the kitten a bath. Younger cats are more likely to accept the concept of bathing and other grooming activities than older cats that have never been exposed to these simple tasks.

BRUSH FIRST!
Always brush a longhaired cat before bathing it. Any mats in the coat will be significantly harder to remove once the hair has become wet.

KEEP A COMB AND BRUSH CLOSE

Keeping a comb and brush in an accessible location can make grooming a cat easier if your pet normally resists this task. Wait until the cat stretches out for a nap, and then reach for the grooming tools. You may only be able to complete a small amount of grooming each day this way, but you will not have to chase your pet before you can begin. Since the cat is tired, it may also be more relaxed during grooming.

Naptime is a good time to groom a reluctant cat.

GIVE YOUR CAT A BREAK

There is no rule stating that you must brush a cat in a single sitting. Do try to end each grooming session on a positive note, though. When you are finished, praise your pet and offer it a treat. Doing so will help the cat to think of grooming as a pleasant activity.

GROOMING GLOVE

If a cat does not seem to like a conventional brush, try using a grooming glove instead. Although it is usually not enough for a longhaired cat, this convenient rubber tool can work wonders on a shorthaired pet. As the name implies, it fits right over the hand. The knobby underside helps to remove dead hair from the cat's undercoat.

GROOMING REX AND HAIRLESS CATS

✿ Rex cats have a very short layer of wavy fur. Grooming with a comb and brush could scratch the cat's skin, but its fur can be wiped with a chamois leather to keep it soft and silky.

✿ A few breeds, such as the Sphynx, are virtually hairless, although they do have a down of fine fur on the face, ears, paws, and tail. The skin should be washed with warm water and a sponge.

It's a Boy!

Nearly all orange cats are male. All orange cats are tabbies, but sometimes the markings are so subtle that the coat appears to be solid-colored.

It's a Girl!

Nearly all calico and tortoiseshell cats are female. When male cats are born with this coloring, they are usually sterile. A tortoiseshell is also called a money cat, because it is thought to bring good fortune.

TORTIES AND TORBIES

- Tortie = A convenient name for a tortoiseshell.
- Torbie = A mixture of tortoiseshell and tabby patterns; also known as a patched tabby.

HOW'S YOUR TOLERANCE?

Most people who suffer from pet allergies are allergic to other things as well. However, the better you can control your reaction to other allergens, the better you will be able to tolerate a feline friend.

❖ A slight cat allergy can be exacerbated by the presence of another offender, such as dust, mold, or pollen. You may be able to lessen your reaction to cats by keeping other allergens to a minimum.

❖ If you have carpets, clean them regularly using a vacuum fitted with a HEPA (high-efficiency particulate air) filter. Better yet, opt for wood flooring, which does not trap allergens in the way that carpeting does.

❖ Take an antihistamine to reduce hay fever symptoms.

Allergies Galore

People with cat allergies outnumber people with dog allergies by a ratio of 2 to 1.

Catnip

Many cats find the scent of catnip extremely tantalizing. If you offer this plant-based treat, be prepared for the cat to sniff it, roll around on its back, and purr with total abandon. Rest assured that your pet will return to normal shortly, with no lingering effects. Catnip is neither dangerous nor addictive.

Catnip
(Nepeta
cataria)

ACTIVE INGREDIENT

The active ingredient that gives catnip its potent effect is called nepetalactone. This organic compound is also extremely effective at repelling mosquitoes.

Catnip Caution

The herb catnip is to some cats what a glass of wine is to humans. It intoxicates them. Although catnip is inherently safe for a cat, it is important that you use caution if you own more than one cat. Individual cats can react in remarkably different ways to this substance. Some cats, particularly males, may go from being an easygoing household member to an aggressive troublemaker with no warning at all when given catnip. To make sure that your cats are happy catnip connoisseurs, always give each cat its first bit of the herb away from all other animals in the home. If a cat becomes hostile when given catnip, it is best not to give it to your pet again.

Age Matters
Kittens less than six months of age and extremely elderly cats usually do not respond to catnip.

MODERATION IS KEY

Avoid giving your pet catnip more than once a week. Although the cat will not be harmed by catnip or become addicted to it, your pet can build a tolerance for the substance. If this happens, the cat will become immune to the herb.

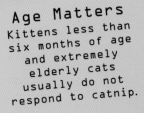

I know it's got catnip in it, but would you want to play with the same toy every day?

A Dirty Job

Mother cats do virtually everything for their kittens for the first two or three weeks of their lives. After the kittens nurse, the mother cat licks the kittens to stimulate elimination. She then swallows the waste and continues licking her young to keep them and the whelping box clean.

LONGHAIRED BREEDS

- American Curl
- Balinese
- Birman
- Chantilly/Tiffany
- Cymric
- Himalayan
- Javanese
- Maine Coon
- Norwegian Forest Cat
- Persian
- Ragdoll
- Scottish Fold
- Siberian
- Somali
- Turkish Angora
- Turkish Van

A mother cat grooming her kitten.

A CAT OF MANY NAMES

This single breed is known by three different names:

Name of Cat	Place or Organization
Pointed Pattern Persian	Cat Fanciers' Association
Himalayan	United States
Colorpoint Longhair	Europe

The Himalayan is a Persian with Siamese colorpoint markings.

NATIVE CATS

Cats are not native to Australia, but marsupials (which have pouches to carry their young) have evolved to fill the same predatory niche. Some marsupials are described as "native cats," although they are unrelated to cats and differ significantly. The tiger quoll or spotted-tailed quoll (Dasyurus maculatus), a typical member of this group, is sometimes referred to as the tiger cat.

CONSIDER AN INDOOR CRATE

In addition to a pet carrier, you may want to purchase an indoor crate for your cat.

✳ Unlike a dog crate, a crate for a cat needs to be large enough to accommodate a bed, dishes, a litter box, and at least a few toys. A dual-level wire model affords a cat with sufficient space as well as opportunities for socialization.

✳ If you have multiple pets, crates can be helpful for separating them at feeding times, bedtime, or when minor altercations arise.

✳ A crate can serve as an excellent tool for gradually familiarizing a timid cat to a new environment, or for introducing the most gregarious cat to an overly excited dog.

✳ A crate can also be useful for keeping kittens out of danger when they cannot be supervised.

Tiger
cat

Tail in the Air
The cat is the only animal species that can walk while holding its tail upright.

ALLERGIES
Approximately 15 percent of cats suffer from some sort of allergy.

Cartoon Cats

Cats have starred in numerous comic strips and animations. Here are a few of the most well-known cartoon felines:

Balloon of Felix the Cat in a zoot suit at a New Year's Day parade.

✪ **Felix the Cat:** Created by Pat Sullivan and animated by Otto Messmer, Felix made his debut in 1919 in Paramount's *Feline Follies* under the name Master Tom. With huge eyes and a giant grin, Felix went on to star in his own comic strip in 1923 and became one of the most popular cartoon cats of the 1920s.

✪ **Sylvester the Cat:** In 1945, Friz Freleng created the character Sylvester the Cat for the cartoon *Life with Feathers*. Uttered in his signature lisp, Sylvester's first words were "Thufferin' Thuccotash." Mel Blanc, who was the voice of numerous cartoon characters, used the same voice for Sylvester as he did for Daffy Duck, only for Sylvester he spoke faster. In 1947, Sylvester was paired with another character, Tweety Bird. Sylvester has spent numerous decades trying to devour this tiny yellow bird that inevitably outsmarts him every time.

✪ **Top Cat:** Created by the Hanna-Barbera studio, Top Cat (or T.C. to his friends) was introduced on the ABC television network in 1961. The streetwise cat lived in a garbage can in a New York alley with his five feline friends. While embarking on one scam after another, T.C. frequently has to talk his way out of trouble with local cop Officer Dibble.

✪ **Garfield:** Cartoonist Jim Davis introduced Garfield to the world in a syndicated comic strip in 1978. The comic strip now appears in over 2,500 newspapers and is read by more than 250 million people around the world every day. The lazy, lasagna-loving feline made the pounce from funny papers to the television screen in 1988 with *Garfield and Friends*. In 2004, the famous fat cat starred in his first feature film, *Garfield: The Movie*. The sequel, *Garfield: A Tale of Two Kitties*, was released two years later.

Garfield sand sculpture in Portugal.

No Pretenses
"Way down deep, we're all motivated by the same urges. Cats have the courage to live by them."
Jim Davis

SI AND AM

These twin Siamese cats play a memorable supporting role in the 1955 Disney movie *Lady and the Tramp*. They terrorize the goldfish and canary, attempt to steal the baby's milk—and frame the dog for their mischief. Both cats were voiced by singer/songwriter Peggy Lee.

Jerry

Tom

TOM (AND JERRY)

Cat and mouse rivals Tom and Jerry were created by the animation duo Bill Hanna and Joe Barbera in 1940. Although the characters hardly ever spoke, the infamous cat and mouse won seven Academy Awards between 1943 and 1953—more than any other animated series. The Simpsons characters Itchy and Scratchy were created in 1988 in the likeness of this classic cartoon pair.

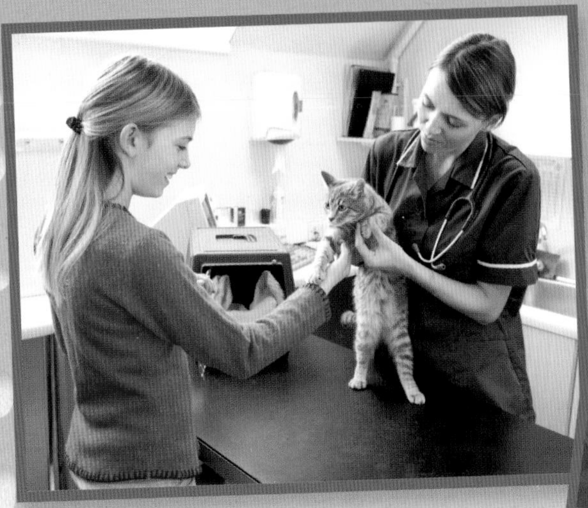

Some veterinarians have a special affinity with cats.

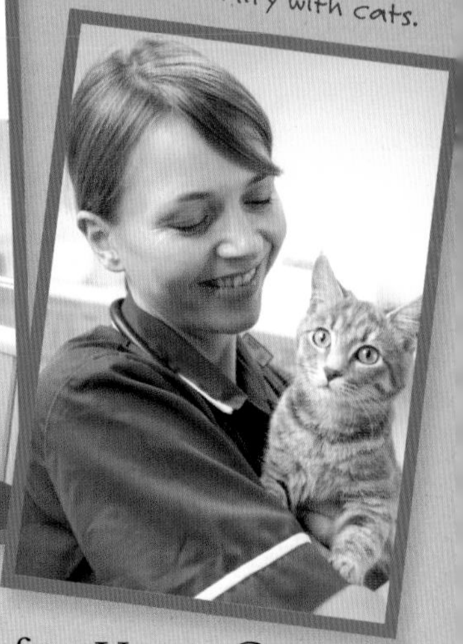

Selecting the Right Vet for Your Cat

It is very important that you are comfortable with the veterinarian you choose for your cat. Not only should you like the cat's doctor, but your pet should be comfortable with this person as well. Selecting the right vet can mean the difference between pleasant checkups and hair-raising struggles whenever it is time for an exam.

- Most veterinarians love animals, but you may prefer a doctor with a particular fondness for cats. A vet who owns cats is going to be even more in tune with this species' idiosyncrasies. Personal experience is often the best teacher.
- You can save yourself a lot of time by checking out the websites of the veterinary practices in your area. Although some vets have yet to make their way to the internet, most have at least a basic site with standard information for potential clients. You may find locations and directions, hospital hours, and staff profiles online. Some sites even include the prices for basic services.
- Some owners prefer a practice that offers separate feline and canine waiting rooms. This feature may be important to you if your cat is especially fearful of dogs. An even better system, however, is a separate waiting room for sick patients and another for animals visiting for wellness exams. After all, you take the cat to the vet to keep it healthy, not to expose it to illness.
- Once you have narrowed the choice down to one or two veterinary practices, stop by each one to get an idea of how it runs. You may even be able to schedule a tour. If you get a bad feeling about a place, keep looking. Whichever veterinary hospital you go with, it should be neat and well organized, with a friendly, knowledgeable staff.

DO CATS HAVE COLLARBONES?

It is a common misconception that cats do not have collarbones. Many people think that cats are so flexible and nimble because they lack a clavicle, but the truth is that their collarbone is simply free-floating. It does not connect with the other bones in the body in the way that people's bones do. Having non-rigid shoulders allows cats to fit through any space that accommodates their head. It also helps them to twist their bodies quickly so that they can land on their feet, although it is a myth that cats can do this every time.

THE CAT YOGA POSE

The cat pose is one of the fundamental yoga postures. It mimics some of the movements of a cat stretching itself—arching and then dipping the back—and is used to keep the human spine supple. As well as benefiting the spine and the trunk, it is also a pleasing, sensuous movement that makes you feel good—just like a cat does when it stretches.

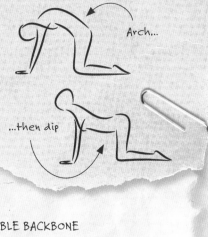

Arch,...

...then dip

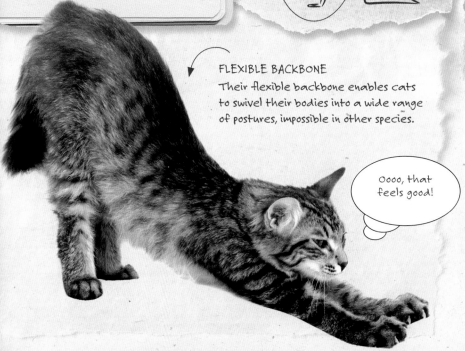

FLEXIBLE BACKBONE
Their flexible backbone enables cats to swivel their bodies into a wide range of postures, impossible in other species.

Oooo, that feels good!

PETERBALD
Adult Peterbald cats are virtually hairless, but they are not born that way. It can take up to two years for this breed to lose its hair.

WRINKLES

Hairless cats appear to have extremely wrinkly skin. In actuality, these bald breeds have no more wrinkles than other cats—most cats have fur to cover the wrinkles, so we just don't see them.

WHY DO CATS RUB AGAINST US?

Cats have scent glands on various body parts, including the face and paws. Cats release these scents, called pheromones, when they rub against furniture and other household items as a means of marking their territory. When a cat rubs against you, it is claiming you in a similar way. You may notice that your pet performs this gesture whenever you have been in the presence of another animal. You may have forgotten about the dog that you saw at the park this morning, but the cat can still smell its scent on your clothes.

THERE'S THE RUB

* *You can purchase a synthetic version of the natural chemical that a cat uses to mark its family and surroundings through face rubbing.*

* *Applying this product around the home may make a cat feel more secure. By infusing the home with these pheromones, you also lessen the cat's desire to claim territory by marking it with urine. Cats rarely spray over an area marked with face hormones.*

* *If the cat has already begun urine-marking behavior, synthetic pheromones can help to fix the problem. You must clean all surfaces completely before applying the product, because the cat will smell any traces of urine left behind and continue to spray mark if you do not clean thoroughly.*

Is Exercise Okay for a Pregnant Cat?

Yes! An expectant mother needs exercise just like any
other cat. In fact, getting regular exercise throughout
the gestational period will make her delivery easier.
Owners should, however, limit the amount of jumping
a pregnant cat does from high places. A fall could be
dangerous for both her and her kittens.

LEFT, THEN RIGHT

When cats walk, they move
both their left feet and then both
their right feet. The only other
animals that move this way
are camels and giraffes.

FELINE FIRST-AID KIT

Keep the following items on hand at all times:

❏ Antibiotic ointment

❏ Antiseptic solution
   or spray

❏ Any medications that
   the cat takes

❏ Blanket

❏ Contact information for
   the nearest emergency
   veterinary hospital and
   your regular vet

❏ Conforming bandage

❏ Cotton balls

❏ Gauze

❏ Elastic bandage

❏ Elizabethan collar

❏ Emergency ice pack

❏ Hydrocortisone cream

❏ Hydrogen peroxide

❏ Magnifying glass
   (preferably one with
   a light)

❏ Medicinal liquid paraffin

❏ Saline solution

❏ Scissors

❏ Small flashlight
   (with extra batteries)

❏ Styptic powder or pencil

❏ Syringe (needleless)

❏ Thermometer

❏ Tweezers

DOMESTIC CAT CLASSIFICATION

Kingdom . . . . . . Animalia
Phylum . . . . Chordata
Class . . . . Mammalia
Order . . . . Carnivora
Family . . . . Felidae
Genus . . . . Felis
Species . . . . . . Felis catus

The reflective effect known as night shine.

Shiny!

A cat's eyes may seem to glow at night. The animal's retina creates a mirror effect when a flash of light hits the eye after the cat has been in the dark long enough for the pupil to open completely. This reflective quality is referred to as night shine.

CATSEYE ROAD STUDS

Reflective markers are now used as safety devices on roads all over the world. They are designed to reflect automobile headlights at night, so that drivers can navigate the roads safely. The first type of reflective marker was invented by Percy Shaw of England and patented in 1934, consisting of a raised dome housing a pair of reflectors. Producing an effect similar to the reflective shine of a cat's eyes, he named his invention catseyes.

Cat's Eye Nebula

Situated 3,000 light years away, the Cat's Eye Nebula is one of the most complex known planetary nebulae. The nebula is formed by glowing clouds of gas ejected from a dying star.

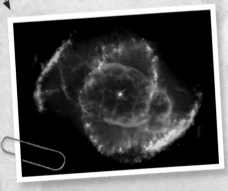

Cymophane

Cymophane is an opalescent form of the gemstone chesoberyl, and is popularly known as cat's eye.

OWNING CATS
AND BIRDS

Owning cats and birds can be risky business, especially when the cat possesses a strong hunting instinct. In many cases, however, the two species can indeed cohabitate peacefully, provided that the owners take a few sensible precautions.

☆ Most importantly, an owner must never allow the bird out of its cage unless the cat is inside a crate, in another room with the door closed, or outside. Even if the cat has shown virtually no interest in birds, this could change in the blink of an eye when the temptation is flying right past your feline companion's face.

☆ Some cats can learn to behave well around birds in cages. Be sure that the cage has a secure clasp that cannot be opened by a clever cat, though. The cage bars should be spaced close enough together to keep out paws and claws.

☆ If you have a larger bird, such as a macaw or cockatoo, you must be equally concerned about both animals' safety. The larger parrots can bite off a cat's paw if the cat puts it where it does not belong. To avoid a horrifying accident such as this, it is best to keep cats and large parrots completely separated at all times.

CATS AROUND THE WORLD

- Albanian—macë
- Arabic—kitte
- Bulgarian—kotka
- Croatian—macka
- Czech—kocka
- Danish— kat
- Dutch—kat
- English—cat
- Finnish—kissa
- French—chat
- German—katze
- Greek—catta
- Hawaiian—popoki
- Italian—gatto
- Norwegian—katt
- Polish—kot
- Portuguese—gato
- Russian—kot
- Spanish—gato
- Swedish—katt
- Turkish—kedi

Gatus   105 PTAS

On Their Toes

Cats are classified as digitigrade animals, meaning that they walk on their toes. They retract their front claws when they walk, but they usually leave their back claws out. Walking this way wears the back claws down, but it allows the front ones to remain as sharp as knives unless they are trimmed regularly.

Retracted claw

Extended claw

Use a blanket or towel if your cat digs its claws in when being petted.

YOU LOOK JUST LIKE…

The word "tabby" likely derives from the name Attabiyah, a neighborhood in Baghdad, Iraq. The markings of tabby cats resemble the wavy patterns of striped silk made in this area.

Digging In

If a cat digs its claws into you when it sits in your lap, place a thick towel or folded blanket under your pet to protect yourself from getting scratched. Most cats dig their claws into whatever surface they are seated upon when they are being petted. Some dig deeply, while others barely dig at all. Resist the urge to reprimand the cat for this normal feline behavior. Your pet will not understand why you are upset, and moreover, you will not be able to prevent this natural reaction.

HAIRBALLS

The expulsion of hairballs is a normal occurrence in cats, especially longhaired ones. The occasional hairball is not a cause for concern, but sometimes digested hair can cause intestinal problems. In extreme situations, surgery may even be necessary to remove a blockage. If a cat is vomiting hairballs frequently or in large amounts, talk to a veterinarian about giving your pet liquid paraffin during times of excessive shedding. Regular grooming is also extremely important for cats prone to persistent hairballs.

Look It Up!
The technical term for a hairball is a bezoar.

Queen Elizabeth I

Elizabethan collar

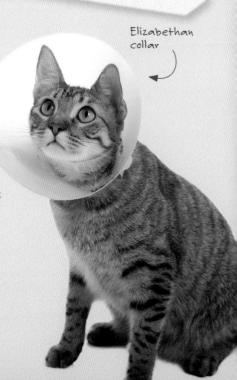

ELIZABETHAN COLLARS

Many cats will lick the site of a surgical incision to the point of causing an infection. You can prevent a cat from licking this or any other type of wound by using an Elizabethan collar. Thus named because it resembles the fashion attire of 16th-century Elizabethan England, these ingenious devices provide a physical barrier between the cat and off-limits areas of its body. Some owners also find these collars useful for stopping excessive scratching. A vet may send you home with a collar following an operation, or you can purchase one from a pet supply store.

Nutritional Requirements

If cats do not receive a well-balanced diet, it will show in their appearance and could lead to serious illnesses. Consult a veterinarian if you are unsure whether your cat is getting the nutrients it requires.

✳ **Proteins:** Cats that eat diets comprised of less than 19 percent protein are at risk of suffering from amino acid deficiencies. A cat consuming a diet that is between 19 and 25 percent protein will still fall short of its required protein intake. This often prompts cats to overeat in an effort to get just a little more of the nutrient. In order for a neutered cat to remain healthy and trim, make sure that its diet is at least 25 percent protein; an intact cat's diet should consist of 35–40 percent protein.

✳ **Fats:** Fats have acquired a bad reputation over the years, but the truth is that all animals need a certain amount of this nutrient in their diets. Too much fat is unhealthy, of course. An excessive amount leads to obesity and places cats at increased risk for multiple diseases. Without any fats, however, a cat would not be able to absorb key vitamins like A, D, E, and K. Fats also give the cat energy and keep its skin healthy and its coat glossy. One of the best things that fats do is to add taste and texture to food—this may seem like a fringe benefit, but bear in mind that a cat cannot get any nutrients from its diet if it will not eat the food. A healthy diet for a cat should include 25–40 percent fat.

✳ **Carbohydrates:** While cats can eat carbohydrates, they do not need these starches and sugars in their diet. Dogs can utilize certain carbohydrates for energy, but cats rely on protein and fat for their energy requirements. Cats that eat too many carbohydrates are at greater risk for obesity and diabetes.

Supplements

If you feed a healthy cat high-quality food, it is not necessary to supplement its diet with vitamins or minerals. If you are concerned that the cat is not getting enough of a particular nutrient, talk to a veterinarian. Never give any animal, healthy or otherwise, any supplement without first checking with a vet.

Proteins and fats should form the basis of a cat's diet.

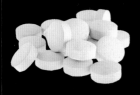

VITAMINS AND MINERALS THAT CATS NEED

Fat-soluble vitamins:
• Vitamin A (retinol)
• Vitamin D
• Vitamin E
• Vitamin K

Unlike a person, a cat synthesizes vitamin C, so it does not need to eat food containing it.

Water-soluble vitamins:
• Niacin
• Pyridoxine
• Roboflavin
• Thiamine

These are part of the B-complex vitamin group.

Minerals:
• Calcium
• Copper
• Iodine
• Iron
• Magnesium
• Manganese
• Phosphorus
• Potassium
• Selenium
• Sodium and chloride
• Zinc

CATS ARE CARNIVORES

Cats need meat in their diet due to their high protein requirement. An amino acid called taurine is of particular concern. Found exclusively in animal-based proteins, taurine helps the cat to maintain healthy digestion, heart function, and vision. It also boosts the cat's immune system. Most mammals manufacture taurine from the other amino acids that they consume. However, cats cannot perform this bodily function to a high enough degree, so they need to obtain sufficient taurine from the meat in their diet.

Cats—wild and domestic—are now the only widespread group of true carnivores left on earth, still eating an almost exclusively meat diet.

IS RAW FOOD SAFE?

Raw diets have become increasingly popular in recent years, but are they safe?

❖ Many cat breeders and owners insist that their animals thrive on raw regimens. They cite improved coat condition, increased vitality, and better overall health as the obvious benefits of raw food.

❖ Some veterinarians also recommend raw feeding plans, but an overwhelming number of them discourage owners from feeding cats and dogs raw food. These critics see the health risks as outweighing any benefits.

❖ Raw food is deficient in calcium, phosphorus, and other vitamins and minerals that cats need to remain healthy. It can also contain dangerous bacteria like E. coli and salmonella. In addition to the risks these bacteria pose to a cat's health, handling tainted food can make you and other household members very sick.

Cats in Space

In 1978, Disney released *The Cat from Outer Space*, a comedic movie about a feline spaceship pilot from another planet who becomes stranded on Earth. The premise was preposterous, but 15 years earlier in 1963, France had actually sent the first cat into space. Her name was Félicette, but some referred to her as Astrocat. Impressively, she survived the trip. A second unnamed cat was launched into space shortly after Félicette, but did not survive.

Remember that a cat,...   ...can never be trusted around mice!

DON'T TRUST YOUR CAT!

Even if a cat appears to have no predatory impulses, never trust your pet around small animals like hamsters, mice, and gerbils. Even the most docile cat is bound to get in touch with its inner hunter when exposed to rodents. It is possible to keep cats and these smaller animals in the same household, but consistent vigilance on the owner's behalf is a necessity. Never allow a pet rodent outside its cage unless the cat is placed securely in a cage of its own or behind a securely closed door.

On Curiosity
"An ordinary kitten will ask more questions than any five-year-old."
Carl Van Vechten

TAKING THE LEAD

✱ *If you choose to walk your cat on a leash, be sure to use a harness instead of a collar. Collars may be fashionable and practical for holding identification tags or bells, but most cats can slip a collar right over their head while walking on a leash. A harness, however, is designed to fit securely and keep the cat safe. Look for an adjustable harness and a lightweight leash.*

✱ *Begin by placing just the harness on the cat. This will allow your pet some time to get used to how it feels before adding the leash. Once the cat seems relatively comfortable with the harness, attach the leash. Again, take it slow. Let the cat walk around wearing the leash before picking up the handle or heading outdoors. Always supervise your pet when the leash is attached, however, because it could become caught on something.*

Use a leash with a harness for walking cats.

SMELLY CAT

On the hit television show *Friends*, Lisa Kudrow's character, Phoebe Buffay, was an aspiring singer/songwriter. Her best-known song, "Smelly Cat," became a jingle for a cat litter company in one episode.

Confidence With a Tail
"Cats invented self-esteem."
Erma Bombeck

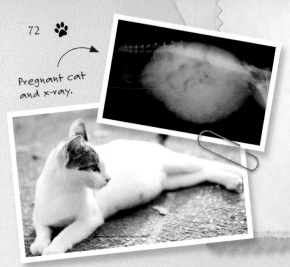

Pregnant cat and x-ray.

DUE DATE

The gestation period for a cat is 63 days. Like people, however, cats may go into labor slightly before or after their due date. If a cat is expecting kittens, she could deliver them anytime between the 57th and 70th day of her pregnancy.

Artemis and Diana

☆ Artemis was the Greek goddess of the moon, and was associated with hunting. The Greek gods lived on Mount Olympus, but when they were threatened by the monster Typhon, they fled in fear to Egypt. However, they were afraid that Typhon would find them, so they assumed disguises in order to hide from him. Each god took the form of an animal; Artemis transformed herself into a cat.

☆ The Romans adopted Artemis and transformed her into the moon goddess Diana, who could take the form of a cat when she needed to flee. In 1899, American folklorist Charles Leland wrote about a group of Diana-worshipping witches in Italy. According to their lore, Diana took the form of her brother's favorite cat in order to trick him into sleeping with her. After resuming her normal form to mate with him, they produced a daughter, Aradia, who was a teacher of witchcraft.

Artemis/Diana, goddess of hunting.

A cat's instinct to bury its feces makes litter box training easy.

WHY DO CATS BURY THEIR POOP?

Cats have a natural instinct that causes them to bury their feces as soon as they eliminate. This is why most cats are so easy to litter box train. Outdoor cats seek out sandy areas when they need to void their bowels, so that they can cover the excrement. Indoor cats also seek a sandy area, and inside the home, this area is inevitably limited to a litter box.

AFFECTIONATE BREEDS

♥ Abyssinian

♥ American Curl

♥ American Wirehair

♥ Balinese

♥ Birman

♥ Burmese

♥ Chantilly/Tiffany

♥ Cornish Rex

♥ Devon Rex

♥ Exotic Shorthair

♥ Havana Brown

♥ Himalayan

♥ Japanese Bobtail

♥ Javanese

♥ Korat

♥ Maine Coon

♥ Manx

♥ Norwegian Forest Cat

♥ Ocicat

♥ Oriental Shorthair

♥ Persian

♥ Ragdoll

♥ Siamese

♥ Singapura

♥ Snowshoe

♥ Somali

♥ Sphynx

♥ Turkish Angora

♥ Turkish Van

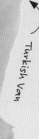

Turkish Van

VAN MARKINGS

The markings of the Turkish Van are responsible for the "van" designation in other cats that are mostly white, with small and discrete areas of color.

TAKING THE PLUNGE

❖ It is generally believed that cats dislike water, but in fact many wild cats are powerful swimmers and will enter water readily. The domestic cat will also tolerate and may sometimes enjoy water. Cats will go outside in the rain and will play with a dripping faucet by pawing at the water as it falls. It is partly a matter of conditioning, since cats that become used to water when young are far less fearful of being bathed, for example, than those that have never had this experience.

❖ One breed of domestic cat, the Turkish Van, is known for liking water. It originates from the vicinity of Lake Van, in Turkey, where these cats will readily swim in the fresh water. The temperature in this part of the world can become very hot in the summer, and it could be that the cats swim as a means of cooling down.

Chaucer's
Manciple

Cats in Literature

Cats have appeared in thousands of factual, fictional, and poetic works of literature. Here are some examples:

✦ "Mice Before Milk," a poem in "The Manciple's Tale," one of the stories in *The Canterbury Tales* (14th century) by Geoffrey Chaucer.

✦ "The Kitten and Falling Leaves" (1807), a poem by William Wordsworth.

✦ "The Black Cat" (1843), a short story by Edgar Allan Poe.

✦ "The Cat That Walked By Himself," one of the *Just So Stories for Little Children* (1902) by Rudyard Kipling.

✦ "The Cat and the Moon," from *The Wild Swans at Coole* (1919) collection of poems by W.B. Yeats.

✦ "Cat in the Rain," from the short story collection *In Our Time* (1925) by Ernest Hemingway.

Mice Before Milk

"Let take a cat, and foster him well with milk
And tender flesh, and make his couch of silk,
And let him see a mouse go by the wall
Anon he waiveth milk and flesh and all
And every dainty that is in that house,
Such an appetite has he to eat a mouse."

EARLY CAT BOOKS

✳ One of the earliest known books to focus on cats is *Beware the Cat*, written by English satirist William Baldwin in the mid-16th century. It is the earliest known piece of original long prose fiction in English, and is therefore a candidate for being the first English novel. The story revolves around tales of cats that can speak and reason, and is in fact an anti-Catholic satire.

✳ French writer and poet François-Augustin Paradis de Moncrif published *Histoire des Chats* in 1727, now considered to be the first great book devoted to cats. The book was a defense of cats using historical references, such as the veneration of cats in ancient Egypt. Although written as a parody of pedantic scholarship, Moncrif was ridiculed by his peers. During Moncrif's induction ceremony into the Académie Française, someone released a cat and the whole audience meowed and laughed.

A cat from Moncrif's
Histoire des Chats.

A production of the stage musical *Cats* in Moscow, Russia.

CAT-OWNING AUTHORS

- Brontë sisters
- Lord Byron
- Charles Dickens
- Ernest Hemingway
- Victor Hugo
- Henry James
- Dr. Samuel Johnson
- Ogden Nash
- Edgar Allan Poe
- Sir Walter Scott
- George Bernard Shaw
- Mark Twain
- Jules Verne
- William Wordsworth

"MEMORY, ALL ALONE IN THE MOONLIGHT…"

Andrew Lloyd Webber's wildly successful stage musical *Cats* was based on a collection of poems by T.S. Eliot entitled *Old Possum's Book of Practical Cats* (1939).

On Character

"If man could be crossed with the cat it would improve man, but it would deteriorate the cat."
Mark Twain

LOOK AWAY

* Cats do not like it when people or other animals stare at them. In the wild, this gesture is considered confrontational.

* When a cat makes eye contact unintentionally, it will blink and look away instantly. If a cat's eyes meet yours when you are looking at it, try mimicking this common feline reaction. Doing so will likely make the cat feel more at ease.

* Some cats will narrow or close their eyes in response to stress.

Cats seem to think that if they cannot see, then they cannot be seen.

I'm a special cat. I can wink as well as blink.

A MATTER OF LOGIC

Cats have a reputation for seeking out the laps of people who like them the least. Some people think that this is the cat's way of putting critics in their place. Do cats indeed have a sixth sense for knowing who does and does not like them? Perhaps, but do they actually try to assert their revenge by forcing themselves on these people? No one can say for certain, but the reason for this common behavior is probably far more logical than emotional. Cats dislike it when people stare at them, so if a room is filled with numerous cat fanciers and only one person who dislikes cats, the individual most likely to avert his or her eyes from the cat is the non-cat person. The cat therefore finds this particular human the least threatening.

Turn On Your Blinker

Here is a fun game to play with a cat. It is also a great way to avoid staring at your pet. When the cat catches your eye, slowly blink. Many cats seem to enjoy it when people do this. Some will even mirror the gesture by blinking in response.

Joking Around

What is the difference between a cat and a comma?

Answer: One has the paws before the claws and the other has the clause before the pause.

Why don't cats play poker in the jungle?

Answer: Too many cheetahs.

What do you get when you cross a chick with an alley cat?

Answer: A peeping tom.

Double Paws

Most cats have a total of 18 toes, with five on each of their front paws and four on each of their back paws. Polydactyl cats have up to seven toes, usually on the front paws only. Although they do not technically have twice as many toes, these cats are said to have double paws. It is estimated that less than 10 percent of any given cat breed are polydactyls, but many of the first cats to arrive along the east coast of North America carried this genetic mutation. With a limited number of breeding specimens in this area, the number of double-pawed cats therefore increased. Today, there are more polydactyl cats between Boston, Massachusetts, and Halifax, Nova Scotia, than in any other area of the world for this reason.

The northeastern part of the United States is home to the greatest concentration of polydactyl cats.

U.S. President Theodore Roosevelt had a polydactyl cat named Slippers.

ADDING TO YOUR FELINE FAMILY

If you are thinking of adding a second or third cat to your household, you must consider whether this is the best choice for everyone involved. Here are a few questions to ask yourself before getting another cat:

❖ **Why do I want this cat?** The right answers to this question are numerous, but be sure that you want to get a second cat for a sound reason. Buying or adopting an animal because you like its looks, because your kids have been begging for it, or because you are worried that your first cat is lonely is not good enough. You should want the animal.

❖ **Do I have enough time for an additional animal?** You must have enough time to feed, play with, and groom another cat. While cats are rarely demanding pets, they do require a certain amount of their owner's time. If you are too busy for another cat, it is better off with another owner.

❖ **Do I have enough money for another cat?** One more pet does not just mean buying extra food. It means another litter box, another annual veterinary visit, and another round of medications such as flea and tick preventatives.

❖ **Is everyone in favor of adding another pet to the household?** All family members within the home should agree that getting another cat is a good idea. If anyone is against the idea, discuss his or her reasons. Perhaps the naysayer is the person responsible for litter box duty. If so, work out a new plan that is acceptable to everyone involved before moving forward.

❖ **How well will my current cat tolerate the newcomer?** If the cat you already have interacts well with other cats, good. If the cat seems to be craving some feline companionship, great. If, however, you suspect that the cat will be less than thrilled about the new addition, you must take this into consideration. You have made a commitment to the pet you already have, and you must place its welfare at the top of your priority list.

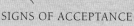

SIGNS OF ACCEPTANCE

If you have added a second or third cat to your household, keep a close eye on all the animals. You will know that they have accepted each other when you find them playing or sleeping together. If you catch one cat grooming another, there is no doubt that they have bonded.

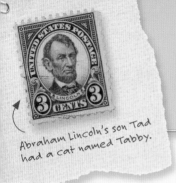

Abraham Lincoln's son Tad had a cat named Tabby.

On Fighting

"No matter how much cats fight, there always seem to be plenty of kittens."
Abraham Lincoln

The Exotic Shorthair is as placid as a Persian but has a coat that is easier to care for.

The Long and the Short of It

The Exotic Shorthair breed is frequently referred to as the lazy man's Persian. Although they are considered separate breeds, the Exotic and the Persian are nearly identical in appearance. The one difference is that the Exotic has a short coat. This thick, dense fur is much easier to groom than the Persian's simply due to its shorter length that keeps it from snarling.

I need daily brushing, but I'm so worth it.

The Persian is one of the oldest breeds of cat, first arriving in Europe from Persia (Iran) in the 16th century and remaining popular ever since.

Asian breeds require lots of attention.

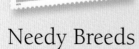

Needy Breeds

Many Asian cat breeds tend to be very dependent. These cats delight in their owner's attention and dislike spending too much time alone. If you plan to buy a Burmese, Balinese, or Siamese cat, consider getting two kittens instead of one for this reason. You need not get two of the same breed, but having feline companionship will make alone time much easier for these breeds.

CROSSED EYES AND KINKED TAILS

Early Siamese cats often had crossed eyes and kinked tails. These traits still exist, although much less commonly. According to folklore, one reason for the kink was that the cats' tails were used by the royalty of Siam for looking after their rings; the tails developed a kink to stop the rings from falling off. Another explanation for both features was that the temple cats of Siam were put in charge of guarding an extremely valuable vase. They took the job very seriously and wrapped their tails tightly around the vase, staring at it so intently that they went cross-eyed.

CROSS PURPOSES

Although many Siamese cats appear to be cross-eyed at first glance, if you continue to watch them you will see that this eye-crossing is usually only temporary. Siamese cats frequently suffer from double vision due to the position of the nerves in the brain that control eyesight. When their vision gets blurry, some cats will cross their eyes in an attempt to correct the problem.

Lilac-point Siamese with crossed eyes.

THERAPY CATS

Therapy cats are trained to visit patients in nursing homes and hospitals with their owners. Spending time with animals has been shown to lower people's stress, anxiety, and even heart rate. A visit from an affectionate feline can also be a welcome break from dealing with a serious illness. The days can be long for an elderly person living in a nursing home, and they can be scary for anyone stuck in a hospital bed. Sometimes, spending a little time petting a cat and listening to it purr is just what the doctor ordered.

Feline company has been proven to be good for health and well-being.

TO YOUR HEALTH

Cat owners are less likely to die from heart problems than people who have never owned a feline pet. According to the National Health and Nutrition Examination Survey, a 20-year study involving nearly 4,500 men and women in the United States, non-cat owners were more than 40 percent more likely to die from a heart attack and 30 percent more likely to die from stroke, heart failure, or other cardiovascular diseases when compared to their cat-owning cohorts.

Questions to Ask a Breeder

❑ **May I have a few references?** Good breeders will not hesitate to provide you with a list of people who have purchased kittens from them in the past. Don't just read the list—call the owners to make sure that they were pleased with both the breeder and the kittens.

❑ **Does the kitten's parents have the appropriate health clearances?** Nearly all breeds are genetically prone to one or two types of health problems. Beware of a breeder who tries to tell you otherwise. What matters is that the breeder has his or her breeding stock tested for these diseases by a relevant veterinary specialist. Ask to see the paperwork.

❑ **Can I meet the parents?** Breeders often use the stud services of other breeders, so you may not be able to meet a kitten's father, but you should be able to meet the mother. Oftentimes, the parents are the best indicators of what a kitten will look and act like as an adult animal.

❑ **Will you provide me with a copy of the litter's pedigree?** This may only be important if you plan to show the cat. Having champions in its family history does not guarantee that a cat will also become a champion, but it definitely does not hurt.

❑ **Is the kitten up to date on all its vaccinations?** You will need to take this health record to the kitten's first veterinary appointment.

❑ **Has the kitten been properly socialized?** It is especially important that kittens are socialized in the early weeks of their lives. Spending time with other cats and people helps a kitten to become comfortable with further social interactions.

❑ **Is the kitten's health guaranteed?** Although the details vary, most breeders provide owners with a written guarantee that the kitten will remain alive and healthy for a certain amount of time. If a kitten develops the health condition to which the breed is prone in the first year, for example, the breeder may offer to provide you with a refund or another animal.

❑ **What type of food has the kitten been eating?** You may not decide to use this food long term, but it is important that you purchase at least some of it for the kitten's first few weeks in its new home.

A good breeder's kittens will be well-socialized and healthy.

REST AND RETRACT
Like most felines, domestic cats retract their claws when they sleep.

Mmmm, I'd love a belly rub. I wonder if anyone will take the hint?

WASH, RINSE, REUSE

Although you might be tempted to top off your cat's food and water each morning, you should make a point of emptying and washing the cat's dishes each and every day. Some cats will not eat food or drink water that has been sitting for too long. Moreover, if the bowls are left unwashed, bacteria can grow rapidly on the surface. These germs can make your pet sick.

Wash your cat's bowls every day.

BEWARE OF THE BELLY

✦ Many people assume that when a cat rolls over, it is exposing its belly in a display of submission. This intention is often the case, but a cat may also roll onto its back so that it can use the claws on all four of its feet. Consider the cat's overall body language for a more reliable idea of its mood.

✦ Until you have gotten to know a cat, refrain from rubbing its belly. This sensitive area is often a cat's least favorite place for someone new to pet it. Some cats may react to the most gentle belly rub by biting or scratching unless they are extremely comfortable with the attention giver.

A Long History

The domestication of cats can be traced back thousands of years to the Middle East.

✤ Genetic studies have revealed that the domestication of cats probably began around 10,000 years ago in the Fertile Crescent region of the Middle East—a lush area encompassing present-day Iraq, Syria, Jordan, Lebanon, and Israel—in conjunction with the development of agriculture. Grain storage near human settlements would have attracted rodents, which in turn would have attracted cats. The cats encouraged to approach people were *Felis sylvestris lybica*, the African wildcat, which populates Africa and the Middle East.

✤ The remains of cats have been found at various prehistoric sites, but it is unknown whether these cats were domesticated. The earliest archeological evidence of domestication comes from a Neolithic grave in Cyprus estimated to be 9,500 years old. Excavations revealed the skeletons of a human and cat laid close together, alongside various tools and other grave objects. The cat closely resembles the African wildcat; wildcats are not indigenous to the island of Cyprus.

✤ The earliest historical records of domestication come from ancient Egypt around 3,500 years ago, including pictorial representations and mummies. Egypt was the greatest grain-growing area of the ancient world, and huge granaries were constructed to store the grain from good harvests for use in leaner years. Cats would have been prized as rodent controllers. Many of the skulls from ancient Egyptian cat cemeteries resemble *F. s. lybica*, while a small proportion is of cats resembling the jungle cat, *F. chaus*. It would appear that the ancient Egyptians tamed both types, but the African wildcat was easily the more popular, and probably more amenable to domestication.

The domestic cat's wild ancestor, the African wildcat, is a lithe animal, similar to a domestic tabby in color.

MATERNAL GENES
Genetic studies show that today's domestic cats can be traced back to at least five female ancestors from the Fertile Crescent region.

An ancient Egyptian carving showing a cat stalking a nest of birds.

NATURE OR NURTURE?

Although cats have a strong instinct to hunt, they do not instinctively know how to do so. Kittens must be taught by their mother. In the wild, a mother cat would bring home real prey to teach her kittens how to hunt, but for domestic cats, a toy mouse is a more acceptable substitute.

Why Do Cats Play With Their Prey?

Many cats play with their prey—batting it around, nearly letting it run away, and then recapturing it. Some cats may even repeat these steps several times before killing the animal. In many cases, this behavior is due to inexperience; other cats are simply poor hunters. Sometimes, however, this proverbial game of cat and mouse has a shrewd purpose, which is to wear the victim out. If the animal can bite, for example, the cat may appear to be playing when it is actually injuring the prey a little at a time before delivering the fatal blow.

Julie Newmar as Catwoman in the 1960s Batman television series, stroking a statue of the Egyptian feline goddess Bastet.

Catwoman

Catwoman—the secret identity of Selina Kyle—appeared in the first self-titled *Batman* comic in 1940 as a burglar and jewel thief called "The Cat."

Catwoman differs from other supervillains in the *Batman* series in that she is also a love interest for Batman, and has even joined forces with him on occasion. Catwoman has been featured in several comic book series, as well as on television and in movies. The following actresses have played the character of Catwoman in the screen versions of the *Batman* saga:

★ **Julie Newmar:** In the first two seasons of the *Batman* TV series (1966–67).

★ **Lee Meriwether:** In the 1966 movie *Batman*.

★ **Eartha Kitt:** In the third and final season of the TV series (1967–68).

★ **Michelle Pfeiffer:** In the 1992 movie *Batman Returns*.

★ **Julia Rose:** In the 2003 television movie *Return to the Batcave: The Misadventures of Adam and Burt*.

★ **Halle Berry:** In the 2004 movie *Catwoman*.

★ **Anne Hathaway:** In the 2012 movie *The Dark Knight Rises*.

Michelle Pfeiffer as Catwoman in the 1992 movie Batman Returns.

The affectionate and inquisitive Birman is also known as the Sacred Cat of Burma.

SACRED CAT

The Birman cat is thought to have originated in Burma. The Kittah priests of this area considered the breed to be a sacred companion. Legend states that when the head priest Mun-Ha was on his deathbed, a cat named Sinh came to his side. When the cat touched the priest, its paws remained white, but the rest of its body suddenly changed color. All of Sinh's other fur became golden brown, and its eyes turned blue—like a golden statue of the blue-eyed goddess Tsun-Kyan-Kse that was housed in the temple. This same transformation then occurred in all the other cats in the monastery. Sinh is considered to be the ancestor of the Birman breed.

Cats at Ground Zero

❧ Eighteen days after the horrific tragedy at the World Trade Center in New York City on September 11th, 2001, a search and rescue dog discovered a tiny survivor among the rubble—a cat named Precious. Although she suffered from multiple injuries, Precious had made it to the roof of one of the buildings, where she was rescued.

❧ In a basement at Ground Zero, another cat was found in a box of paper napkins. Upon closer inspection, the rescuers realized that the box also contained three kittens. The rescuers named the feline mother Hope, as a symbol of what she had given them. Her kittens were christened Freedom, Amber, and Flag.

CATS IN SONGS
- "Alley Cat" by Frank Zappa
- "Black Cat" by Janet Jackson
- "Cat Scratch Fever" by Ted Nugent
- "Cats In The Cradle" by Harry Chapin
- "Cool Cat" by Queen
- "Cool For Cats" by Squeeze
- "Honky Cat" by Elton John
- "The Lovecats" by the Cure
- "Pussy Cat" by Chubby Checker
- "Stray Cat Strut" by Stray Cats
- "What's New Pussycat?" by Tom Jones
- "Year Of The Cat" by Al Stewart

AHHH-CHOO!

According to a Hebrew myth, cats were created when Noah asked God for help with a vermin problem on the ark. It is said that when the male lion sneezed, a cat was expelled from each of his nostrils.

The male lion on Noah's ark gave birth to two cats with a sneeze!

LITTER BOX PROBLEMS

☆ If a cat is urinating outside of its litter box, scented litter could be the reason. The feline nose is much more sensitive than a human's. A smell that you consider mild may be extremely irritating to your pet. If the cat dislikes the scent of its litter, it may look for an alternative location for elimination. If you are concerned about odor, look for an odor-absorbing litter instead of one that merely masks the smell of urine with a stronger scent. Daily cleanings also reduce odors significantly.

☆ Another reason some cats eliminate in places where they should not is that they need an extra litter box. Some cats prefer to urinate in one litter box and defecate in another. You need not place the boxes in different rooms; they can even be side by side. If the cat has such a preference, it will know which box is which and always use the right one.

☆ Cats are extremely clean animals by nature. They prefer not to use a soiled litter box and may even suffer from housetraining regression if they do not have a clean place for elimination. You need at least one litter box for every cat that you own so that each has a clean box to use. An additional box may also be a good idea in case a cat needs to eliminate a second time and will not reuse its litter box if you have not had a chance to clean it out.

☆ If you want to stack the odds of your cat's litter box success in its favor, make it easy for your pet to find a litter box. Place one on every floor of the home.

DO NOT DISTURB! Cats that are interrupted when trying to use their litter boxes are more likely to eliminate where they should not.

Clean out your cat's litter box regularly to avoid problems.

YOUR FIRST PHONE CALL

If your cat has regressed in its litter box training, schedule a veterinary appointment to rule out a physical cause for the problem. Once the veterinarian has given your pet a clean bill of health, you can create a strategy for dealing with the issue from a behavioral standpoint. The vet should be able to help you with this step as well.

Genetic Deafness

In the feline species, there is a close link between deafness and coloration.

❖ About 22 percent of white cats with non-blue eyes are born deaf due to a genetic mutation.

❖ For white cats with one blue eye and one non-blue eye, the percentage rises to 40 percent.

❖ When a cat is born with a white coat and two blue eyes, it has an 85 percent chance of being deaf.

❖ Interestingly, white cats with one blue eye and one yellow eye are often deaf only on the side with the blue eye.

This difference in eye coloration is the result of a relative excess or lack of melanin.

Pick Up Those Pamphlets

When you visit a cat show, be sure to check out the handouts available at the information booth. If you are trying to decide which breed is the best match for you, this educational material just might lead you to the cat of your dreams. Oftentimes, the pamphlets contain contact information of the breeders participating in the show—the worst time to realize that you did not get the name of that fabulous breeder you spoke with is after everyone has gone home. Show flyers may also provide information about basic cat care, common feline health issues, upcoming shows, and even how you can support your local humane society.

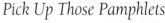

No, I'm not named after a rabbit because I've got big ears. Humans can be so rude!

CLOSE BUT NO CIGAR?

Many cat fanciers believe that the Havana Brown was named after the rich color of a fine Cuban cigar. Historians counter that the breed was named after the brown Havana rabbit, which has the same coloring as this dark feline—and may itself have been named after a Havana cigar.

CAT BREEDER'S DICTIONARY

- Dam—Mother cat
- Sire—Father cat
- Queen—Unspayed female cat
- Tom—Unneutered male cat
- Estrus—Time when a female cat is in heat
- Gestation—Time a female cat is pregnant
- Wean—To move from drinking the dam's milk to eating solid food

DANGEROUS DELIVERY

In 1996, four radioactive kittens were discovered at a power plant in San Onofre, California. It seems that a pregnant cat had found her way inside and delivered her litter there. Luckily, the feline family had a happy ending. All four of the kittens—Alpha, Beta, Gamma, and Neutron—were officially deemed radiation-free seven months after their highly unconventional birth.

> How adorable do I have to look to get adopted around here?

NO-KILL SHELTERS

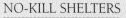

If you plan to adopt a cat from a shelter, you may think that a no-kill shelter is the most humane place to start. After all, most people can only rescue one or two cats—and no one likes to think of what might happen to all the other animals that are not chosen at a regular shelter. The truth is that the cats at mainstream shelters need you far more than the ones at these more selective organizations do. It is important to understand that the reason no-kill shelters can promise never to euthanize their animals is that they will not accept animals that have a poor chance of being adopted. These cats are surrendered to other shelters instead. This fact actually contributes to overcrowding at the regular shelters, which is the biggest cause for the euthanasia of pets that do not find new homes after an extended time period.

The Ragdoll is a placid and loving cat, and loves to play and be petted. It has a thick coat that is easy to groom.

LITTLE DOLLS

✤ It seems fitting that the Ragdoll was given the name of a toy. These popular cats take much longer to mature than other breeds. It can take up to two years for their coats to grow into their adult color, and they often do not reach their full weight and size until they are about four years old.

✤ The Ragdoll got its name from its incredibly relaxed nature. These cats often become so comfortable when given attention that their bodies go limp. It is a myth, however, that Ragdolls are insensitive to pain. They feel pain just like any other cat.

When held, a Ragdoll cat goes as limp as, well, a ragdoll.

CAT SAINTS

Cats were associated with some of the early Christian female saints. One was St. Gertrude of Nivelles, to whom both the cat and the mouse were sacred. Another was St. Agatha, often referred to as Santo Gato (St. Cat). She was said to turn into a fierce cat when she was angered by women who worked on her feast day.

St. Agatha was said to take the form of a fierce cat.

Body Language

A cat's body language can tell you and other cats a lot about how it is feeling. A cat may display some or all of the following signs when it is:

★ **Happy:** Relaxed whiskers, perked-up ears, head and tail held high in the air (or tail waving from side to side in rapid motions if especially excited).

★ **Friendly:** Head and ears stretched forward, whiskers standing straight out from face, hair smooth and flat, tail still and upright (or kept close to body), may greet by meowing or purring.

★ **Content:** Blinking or winking eyes, pupils normal for light level, whiskers relaxed or gently twitching, erect ears, soft purring, rubbing against owner, may be curled into a ball or stretched out on back if sleeping, may purr.

A frightened cat, crouched and staring intently.

★ **Frightened:** Eyes bulging, ears flat against head, whiskers flat against face, hair raised on back and tail, crouched body, tensed muscles, fixed position, bent hind legs, hair standing erect all over body, may growl, hiss, or spit.

★ **Defensive:** Eyes averted, ears bent back, arched back, bent forelegs and hind legs (or a slightly raised paw), thumping tail, raised hair in a narrow line along the spine and tail, may growl, hiss, or spit.

★ **Angry:** Staring eyes, constricted pupils, erect ears, lips curled in a snarl, hair raised on shoulders and tail, tensed body muscles, fixed position, stretched back, tail swinging in low arcs close to the body or in sudden whips, may hiss or screech.

A content cat rubbing against its owner with eyes closed.

An angry cat, with arched back, raised fur, bulging eyes, and hissing.

WHY DO SOME CATS SUCK CLOTH?

Some cats develop a habit of sucking on cloth. Similar to a human child who finds comfort in sucking on a pacifier, the cat uses the cloth as a self-soothing device. A kitten that was weaned too soon from its mother may be prone to this behavior. For some reason, Siamese cats also seem especially susceptible to cloth-sucking, sometimes called wool-sucking. Although merely gnawing on cloth may be harmless, the habit becomes more dangerous when a cat begins eating the material, which can lodge in its intestine and create a potentially fatal blockage. If this happens, swift surgical intervention is necessary. Cloth-sucking can also ruin clothing, linens, and other materials, so even owners dealing with a minor situation may wish to nip the problem in the bud.

When a cat sucks cloth, it is reenacting the behavior of a kitten suckling.

TIPS FOR REDUCING CLOTH-SUCKING

✦ **Limit the cat's access to clothing and linens.** *Keep closet doors and drawers closed, and put away clean laundry immediately. Toss dirty laundry into the hamper instead of leaving it lying around. Since wool is a favorite material of cloth-sucking cats, you might need to be especially careful with knit items.*

✦ **Divert the cat.** *When your pet begins to suck on cloth, remove the item immediately and offer a toy or treat instead. Praise the cat lavishly for accepting the new item.*

✦ **Keep the cat busy and well exercised.** *A cat that gets plenty of stimulation, both physical and mental, is less likely to develop a cloth-sucking habit.*

✦ **Allow the cat one item and keep an eye on it.** *Some owners find it easier to give in to cloth-sucking—at least on a limited scale. If you let the cat have one item of its own, it will be more likely to leave your possessions alone. You must be certain that the cat is not ingesting the material, however. Only allow the cat to have its cloth when you can properly supervise it.*

✦ **Talk to a veterinarian.** *If the cat becomes obsessive about cloth-sucking, talk to a veterinarian about placing your pet on a prescription medication such as an anti-anxiety drug. Also, ask the vet if he or she can recommend an animal behaviorist in your area. Medications can be helpful, but they must be combined with behavior modification techniques in order to achieve the best results.*

DON'T CRY FOR THIS ARGENTINIAN CAT
In Argentina in the late 1940s, a cat named Mincha climbed up a 40-foot (12-m) tree—and essentially stayed there for six years. Mincha gave birth to three litters of kittens while she was living the high life. They were all delivered in her makeshift tree house. Local people fed Mincha by attaching food to long poles.

TYPES OF CAT BED
- Beanbag or padded
- Cardboard box with a blanket
- Hooded or igloo
- Plush or fleece
- Wicker with a cushion
- Radiator or self-warming

No Right or Wrong Way

Some cats sleep on their owner's bed. Others have beds of their own that the owner expects them to use instead. Wherever you stand on the issue of where cats should sleep, you need not worry about defying any hard and fast rules. Even experts often stand on different sides of this decision that every cat owner must make. If your choice works for you, it is the right one. If it does not work for someone else, that is okay—unless the person is your significant other. In this situation, the most practical solution is to get your cat a feline companion, so that no one has to sleep alone.

Many cats like igloo beds because they feel warm and safe.

Low Maintenance, Not No Maintenance

★ Many people think that cats are easy pets. After all, cats do not need daily walks or weekly baths. Most of them do not even care if you leave them alone most of the time, right? Certainly, cats are known for being considerably more independent than dogs—and to some degree this is true. However, thinking that owning a cat means not having to provide it with exercise, grooming, or attention is ridiculous. If you do not have time to care for a pet properly, the best thing you can do is wait until you are in a better position to become a cat owner.

★ The most important thing that a cat needs is love. Spending time with the cat each day and giving it some attention will deepen the bond that the two of you share.

★ Regular checkups at the veterinarian are an important step in keeping a cat healthy, but it is not enough by itself. Cats also need to eat nutritious food and get plenty of exercise to remain in good physical shape.

★ Staying mentally healthy is important. Providing the cat with plenty of toys and making time for interactive play will alleviate boredom, prevent unpleasant behaviors, and keep your pet's mind sharp.

Toys and playtime are important for a cat's well-being.

SCAREDY CATS
Felinophobia is the irrational fear of cats.

There's a Name for It
Ailurophilia is the technical term for the love of cats.

SABER-TOOTHED CATS

The saber-toothed cats that roamed the plateaux and forest regions of prehistoric times were ferocious hunters, capable of hacking down prey with their elongated upper canine teeth. They are believed to have fed on mastodons (primeval elephants). Unlike contemporary cats, saber-toothed cats used their canines for stabbing rather than biting, sinking them deep through the tough hide of the mastodon. They died out about 11,000 years ago, leaving no immediate descendants.

The skull of a saber-toothed cat. To accommodate the huge upper canine teeth, which were used to stab prey and then tear it apart, the jaws of a saber-toothed cat could open to 90 degrees.

Pearly Whites
Domestic cats have a total of 30 teeth— 12 incisors, 10 premolars, 4 canines, and 4 molars.

The Smilodon, which inhabited North and South America, were among the most advanced of the saber-tooths and had the largest canine teeth.

BENEFITS OF STERILIZATION

✤ Spaying and neutering not only help to reduce the animal population, but these simple procedures also help to keep a cat healthy. Sterilization helps to prevent mammary cancer, and completely eliminates the risk of ovarian, uterine, and testicular cancer.

✤ Some people think that females should be allowed to have at least one litter before being fixed. The truth is that cats that are spayed before their first heat cycle are healthier than those spayed later in life. Becoming a mother also does not make a female cat happier.

✤ Other owners worry that neutering a male cat somehow makes him less masculine. This, too, is untrue. A male cat may be less aggressive, more loving, and more consistent about using his litter box if he is sterilized at an early age, but he will also still be a bona fide male.

The Hindu warrior goddess Durga riding a large feline.

Indian Cats

✱ *A Sanskrit document dating from about 1000* B.C.E. *mentions a pet cat.*

✱ *The Indian epics* Ramayana *and* Mahabharata, *dating from about 500* B.C.E., *both contain stories about cats. The Indians at that time worshipped a feline goddess of maternity called Shashti, and for decades Hindus were obliged to take responsibility for feeding at least one cat.*

✱ *Shashti is sometimes regarded as an aspect of Durga, the Hindu warrior goddess. Durga holds a weapon in each of her multiple hands and rides a tiger or lion.*

A female cat can have multiple litters each year. In some areas there are sterilization programs to try to control feral cat populations.

IS IT TOO LATE?

Unless it has a medical issue that makes anesthesia inadvisable, a cat is never too old to be spayed or neutered. Sterilization makes pets less vulnerable to numerous health problems, even when done later in life. Moreover, both male and female cats remain fertile for many years if they are not fixed. While fertility does decline a bit with age, even an elderly female cat can become pregnant.

The cheetah is the fastest land animal alive today.

The Fastest Cat

The cheetah is the supreme athlete of the cat family. It is built for speed, and its relatively long legs give good stride length. The cheetah is unique in the cat family for lacking retracting claws.

The domestic cat—faster than the fastest human.

Akbar the Great

In Asia, it used to be commonplace for cheetahs to be kept and trained for hunting purposes, and they were even exercised on leashes. Akbar the Great (1542–1605), the Mughal emperor of India, maintained an amazing collection of thousands of these animals.

RUN LIKE THE WIND

It is estimated that a domestic cat can run as fast as 30 miles per hour (48 kph) in short bursts of time. When one considers that cheetah can run at speeds of 70 miles per hour (112 kph), your pet feline's abilities probably do not sound impressive, but consider this: Jamaican Olympic medalist Usain Bolt's top recorded speed is 28 miles per hour (45 kph). Kind of puts everything into perspective, doesn't it?

What Is a Cat Breed?

❖ A cat breed is simply a group of cats that share the same physical and behavioral traits. For example, Siamese cats share the same svelte build and long head, while Persian cats are heavy boned with a round head.

❖ Some cat breeds have been created by hybridization—that is, the intentional crossing of two separate breeds. The majority of breeds, however, are the result of nature taking its own course in producing cats with a variety of unique traits—and of breeders then striving to reproduce these qualities consistently in future generations.

❖ More than 100 cat breeds exist, but different cat registries—governing bodies that keep a register of cats and their lineage, and set down rules and regulations for cat shows—officially recognize a different number of them. For example, the Cat Fanciers' Association (CFA) recognizes 41 breeds, while the International Cat Association (TICA) recognizes 55 breeds.

The Persian has a heavyweight (or cobby) body and a large, round head.

The Siamese is a light-boned cat, with a long body, legs, and tail, and a long, wedge-shaped head.

CAT ORGANIZATIONS

✦ American Association of Cat Enthusiasts (AACE)

✦ American Cat Association (ACA)

✦ American Cat Fanciers Association (ACFA)

✦ Australian Cat Federation (ACF)

✦ Canadian Cat Association (CCA)

✦ Cat Fanciers' Association (CFA)

✦ Cat Fanciers Federation (CFF)

✦ Fédération Internationale Féline (FIFe)

✦ Governing Council of the Cat Fancy (GCCF)

✦ Livre Officiel des Origines Félines (LOOF)

✦ National Cat Fanciers' Association (NCFA)

✦ New Zealand Cat Fancy (NZCF)

✦ The International Cat Association (TICA)

✦ Traditional Cat Association (TCA)

✦ United Feline Organization (UFO)

✦ World Cat Federation (WCF)

THIS SIDE UP

It is a common belief that cats can fall from great heights and always land on their feet without injury—this is perhaps where the myth that cats have nine lives comes from. Cats do indeed possess a unique talent for twisting their bodies in the blink of an eye so that they can land paws-down most of the time. However, this ability does not prevent them from getting hurt. Many cats end up in veterinary emergency rooms with broken bones after falls from high places.

BEWARE OF BROKEN BONES
The two most common causes of broken bones in cats are falls and traffic accidents.

GROUND RULES FOR KIDS

Kids and cats can get a great deal of enjoyment from playing together, but it is important to supervise young children when they are playing with a cat.

* Keep the kids and the cat in a designated area. This makes supervising them both much easier.

* If you have small children, establish a rule that the kids can only play with the cat when they are sitting on the floor.

* Provide the children with cat toys, such as feathers or balls with bells, to entice the cat to play, but make it clear that if the cat runs away, the playtime session is over.

* Never allow a toddler or preschooler to chase or carry a cat—kids this young are simply not coordinated enough to hold a cat properly while maintaining their own balance.

It is best if young children play with a cat at ground level, because they could accidentally drop the cat if they pick it up.

A male cat adopting an aggressive stance to intimidate another cat that has come into his territory.

Killer Instincts

Male cats have little to do with the kitten-rearing process. Once mating has occurred, the job of raising the litter is left primarily to the female. A father will defend the territory of his young family, however, if another male gets too close. Male cats have strong instincts when it comes to procreation. Some will even kill kittens that they come into contact with in an effort to carry on their own genes.

Cleopatra

The Face of Beauty

Cleopatra's cat, Charmian, is said to have been the inspiration for the way in which the queen adorned her face with paint and other decorations.

YOU MISSED A SPOT

As a cat gets older, decreased flexibility may make self-grooming a more difficult task. The cat may need some help washing areas such as the back of its neck and the back of its hind legs. Although your pet probably grooms itself several times each day, a quick daily sponge bath from you will be sufficient. Most pet supply stores sell moistened pet wipes that you can use for this purpose. A damp cloth will also work well.

Please don't show a picture of me after I've had a bath. I'll never live it down if any of the neighborhood cats see it!

BATHING YOUR CAT

Cats do not usually need help in keeping their fur clean, but if a cat's coat is particularly dirty or the cat is longhaired, an occasional bath may be necessary. Cats may not like the experience of being bathed at first, but in time, they can become accustomed to it.

1 Fill a basin with about 4 inches (10 cm) of warm water, and gently but firmly place the cat in it. Using a sponge or cup, pour water over the cat's body, avoiding its face and eyes and the top of its head.

2 Gently clean the fur with special cat shampoo. Some owners bathe their pets with human shampoo, thinking that they are spoiling their animals by doing so. However, a cat's skin is less acidic than a human's, so it needs a shampoo with a different pH balance. Human shampoo can leave the cat's skin too dry, encouraging the animal to scratch itself.

3 Rinse the cat with lukewarm water, then carefully lift the cat out of the basin and wrap it in a warm towel. If necessary, clean its head and face with a moistened soft cloth. Towel-dry the cat and keep it in a warm room until completely dry, then brush or comb the fur.

Commercial Cat Foods

Pet food manufacturers have devoted an enormous amount of research to formulating cat food that provides all the vitamins, minerals, and other nutrients required to keep a cat healthy. A good-quality commercial cat food can be used as a complete diet.

WET OR DRY?

Neither type of food is the better option for all cats. Both wet and dry foods have their own advantages. Semi-moist foods offer a middle-of-the-road option, but many formulas are extremely high in sugar.

Dry Food

✦ More economical

✦ More convenient

✦ Keeps teeth cleaner

✦ Stays fresher longer once opened

Wet Food

✦ More appealing scent

✦ Provides hydration as well as nutrition

✦ Lessens the risk of developing urinary problems

✦ Smaller packaging can mean greater variety

Dry food

Wet food

CHANGING FOODS

If you decide to swap your cat to a new food, be sure to do so gradually. Sudden dietary changes can lead to digestive problems, such as stomach upset and diarrhea. Begin by replacing about a quarter of the old food with the new formula. After about a week, change to a mixture of half and half. By the third week, the cat's meals should consist of about three-quarters of the new food. The transition should be complete in a month's time.

Cat Food Only

Do not feed dog food to a cat—or vice versa. Cats and dogs have significantly different nutritional needs.

FREE-FED CATS

If you free-feed an adult cat dry food, it will probably visit its food dish somewhere between 10 and 20 times a day. Wild cats hunt whenever the opportunity arises. Pet cats do not have to find their own food, but they simulate this loose routine by eating at various times throughout the day. If you feed a cat wet food, you may want to divide its daily portion into several servings for this reason.

CONTROVERSIAL INGREDIENTS

Some of the ingredients used in commercial pet foods are contentious.

✤ **Meal and by-products:** Pet food manufacturers use leftovers from the human food industry. Some of these leftovers are rendered (heat processed) to produce meat meal and bone meal. By-products include parts of an animal such as viscera and feet. When cats eat their prey, they eat muscle, skin, bones, and internal organs, but the concern is that some pet foods contain by-products and meal made from by-products that are of variable nutritional quality. When derived from nutritious sources, meat meal is actually a healthy, concentrated source of protein.

✤ **Chemical preservatives:** Synthetic antioxidants, such as butylated hydroxyanisole (BHA), butylated hydroxytoluene (BHT), and ethoxyquin, are added to foods to keep fats from turning rancid. BHA and BHT have been linked to allergic reactions, dental disease, dry skin, and adverse effects on kidney and liver functions. Regular consumption of ethoxyquin has been linked to blindness, leukemia, and cancer of the liver, skin, stomach, and spleen. Some cat owners prefer to use foods preserved with naturally occurring compounds such as tocopherols (vitamin E).

An All-knowing Nose

☆ Don't be surprised if a cat turns up its nose at day-old food. Wet food should be disposed of as soon as the cat has finished eating, but even if you feed your pet dry food, it will prefer a fresh serving over a stale one.

☆ A cat will also probably not eat food that has been treated with any type of medication. The cat's nose is so powerful that it can detect the presence of anything suspicious immediately.

☆ This instinctual ability helps to protect cats from consuming spoiled food. Even in the wild, cats rarely feast on carrion, because their noses tell them that the meat is not fresh.

CARBOHYDRATE CONTENT

❋ Try to feed your pet a good-quality food that contains a high percentage of protein and fat rather than carbs.

❋ If a cat eats any brand of dry food, it is consuming carbohydrates. Dry food cannot be made without carbs, which give dry food its form and texture. Wet food requires no carbohydrates whatsoever, although carbs may be used as ingredients because they are cheaper than meats.

❋ The difference in moisture content between dry and wet food makes it difficult to compare the nutrient percentages between the two types. However, wet cat food generally contains a greater percentage of protein and fat and less carbohydrate than dry food.

A Grave Discovery

**The ancient Egyptians thought so highly of their cats
that they mummified them when they died.**

✤ The center of the Egyptian cult of the feline goddess Bastet was
a city in the Nile delta called Bubastis. Every year, a great festival
would be held and the people would make the pilgrimage along
the Nile to attend. Among other rituals, sacrifices of young cats
would be made.

✤ Bubastis is the site of Egypt's most famous cat cemetery. It seems
that many of the mummified cats that have been unearthed were
the victims of sacrifice, since they had had their necks broken.
Most were young—not yet fully grown—and may well have
been bred especially for this purpose.

✤ In 1888, more than 300,000 mummified cats were discovered
in a cemetery in Bubastis. The remains were unwrapped and
shipped abroad to be used as fertilizer.

ALSO KNOWN AS...

★ Now often referred to as the Aby, the Abyssinian was once known
as the Hare, Bunny, or Rabbit Cat, because it was thought that it
had resulted from a cross between a cat and a wild rabbit. The
Aby has an unusual ticked coat, known as the agouti (or wild-
type) pattern—rather like the ticked coat of a wild rabbit.

★ A popular story about the Abyssinian's origins
relates how, in the 1860s, the emperor of Abyssinia
(modern-day Ethiopia) arrested some British
subjects living in his country after Queen Victoria
failed to respond to his marriage proposal. When
the queen retaliated by sending armed forces, the
emperor shot himself—using a gun that the queen
had given to him as a gift. The story goes that when
the confrontation ended in 1868, a British soldier
brought a female kitten named Zula back home with
him, and it is from Zula that the Abyssinian breed
originates. Unfortunately, no evidence exists to connect
Zula with today's pedigree cats.

Queen
Victoria

The Abyssinian has been referred to
as the Child of the Gods because of
its close resemblance to the sacred
cats of the ancient Egyptians.

Elaborately wrapped ancient Egyptian cat mummies dating from the Late Period, between 715 and 332 B.C.E. The mummy on the left has a decorated headpiece made from stuccoed and painted linen.

Tuxedo coat pattern

Coat Patterns

Coat patterns are different from breeds. Some breeds are available in various coat patterns—for example, a British Shorthair and a Persian may both be tortoiseshell cats.

❁ **Calico:** Black, orange, and white in large blocks across the body.

❁ **Colorpoint:** Light-colored body with dark-colored areas on the head, ears, legs, paws, and tail.

❁ **Particolor:** Consisting of two or more colors.

❁ **Solid (or self-colored):** Consisting of a single color with no markings.

❁ **Tabby:** Striped, blotched, spotted, or ticked.

❁ **Tortoiseshell:** Black, light red, and dark red intermingled and evenly distributed over the body. A cream facial blaze is desirable.

❁ **Tuxedo:** Solid black with the exception of a white bib and white feet.

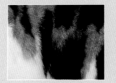

Solid (this example is chocolate)

Particolor (this example is red and white)

Calico

Tortoiseshell

HEAT SENSITIVE

The pigment-producing enzyme in colorpoint cats is heat-sensitive and only activates at cooler temperatures. The cooler extremities of the cat are therefore darker than its warmer body.

Colorpoint (this example is blue pointed)

Blotched tabby

Spotted tabby

Striped tabby

Ticked tabby

Au Naturel
The natural color of the domestic cat is tabby, with striped tabby being the most common.

Questions to Ask a Boarding Facility

Many people are anxious about leaving a pet in a boarding facility, but sometimes there is no other choice. Ask the following questions to help you decide whether a particular boarding facility will be right for your cat:

★ **What are the vaccination requirements?** A business that demands proof of all vaccines mandatory by law is the safest place for your pet.

★ **May I see the boarding area?** The only acceptable answer is yes, but as a courtesy, schedule your visit for a time that is convenient for the business. Refrain from requesting a tour during peak drop-off and pick-up times.

★ **Is the facility clean and well maintained?** No matter how many animals are present, the only smell you should notice is the faint scent of bleach.

★ **How much space will my cat have?** The more space, the better. Tiny quarters mean more animals sharing air space—a situation ripe for the spreading of disease.

★ **Is there proper ventilation?** You want your cat to have fresh air, but watch out for open windows. They pose an escape risk.

★ **Is there an outdoor area for exercise and mental stimulation?** A secure run with a cement floor is ideal, since it is the easiest material to keep clean. Grass, while good for a private outdoor area, cannot be disinfected properly for safe multi-cat use.

★ **Do you board dogs as well as cats?** Many businesses serve both cat and dog owners, but make sure that the one you choose has a separate area for each species. Some dogs can be extremely loud, a fact that can make boarding more stressful for your feline friend if the noise is not buffered.

★ **How do you handle medical emergencies?** There is no single correct answer to this question. Some businesses have veterinarians on site. Others may use a particular emergency clinic if an animal gets injured or becomes sick. What is important is that the facility has a detailed plan and that you are comfortable with this protocol.

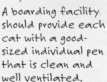

A boarding facility should provide each cat with a good-sized individual pen that is clean and well ventilated.

CATS FROM INDONESIA?

Although the name may lead you to believe that Balinese cats hail from the Indonesian island of Bali, Balinese actually originated in the United States. They received the name due to their graceful movements, which resemble those of Balinese dancers. Similarly, Javanese cats have no connection with the island of Java. The name was chosen for its relationship with Bali and for its exotic sound.

Colorful wooden cat souvenirs from Bali.

BALINESE OR JAVANESE?

When people refer to the Balinese and Javanese breeds, they could be speaking about different cats. Geography can help to narrow things down.

- The Balinese is a longhaired version of the Siamese. In North America, only cats in the four traditional Siamese point colors (seal, blue, chocolate, and lilac) are accepted as Balinese. Elsewhere, any point color and pattern are accepted as Balinese.

- The use of the term Javanese is even more confusing. In North America, the name Javanese refers to Balinese cats that do not match the four traditional Siamese point colors. In New Zealand, Balinese cats with solid-colored or spotted coats are referred to as Javanese.

- In Europe, the Javanese name is reserved for the longhaired version of the Oriental Shorthair, which arose from a breeding program in Britain that strived to re-create the Angora. Just to add to the confusion, the British version of the Javanese is sometimes referred to as the Cuckoo Cat or the Mandarin Cat.

This seal lynx (tabby) point cat would be called a Javanese in the United States but a Balinese elsewhere.

TAKE YOUR BREATH AWAY

Some people still believe that a cat that is allowed to crawl close to the face of a sleeping person can steal his or her breath. This old wives' tale came from the belief that witches could masquerade as cats. As silly as it sounds, many mothers keep cats away from their napping infants to this day, just to err on the side of caution.

Don't believe the myth that a cat can steal a sleeping person's breath.

An orange tabby kitten stretching out its toes and claws.

Gaining Control

Kittens are born with their claws extended. They cannot retract them voluntarily until the muscles in their paws develop more. This is a gradual process that usually concludes when they are around four weeks old.

MOST TOES

Orange tabbies seem to dominate when it comes to the most toes. Jake, an orange tabby from Deep River, New York, has 28 toes. He usurped the title away from another orange tabby named Mickey, who only had 27.

Temporary Home

Many Buddhists believe that the body of a cat is a transient resting place for highly spiritual beings.

CURBING COUNTER SURFING

Cats like to climb up to high places, including counters and tables where you may not wish them to be for hygiene reasons. Here are some tips on how to curb kitty's counter surfing:

❊ Provide the cat with a place for climbing. Many cats enjoy having their own carpeted towers to climb, but a cat may get just as much enjoyment from hanging out on the top bunk in the kids' room.

❊ If you catch the cat on the counter (or dining table), immediately tell your pet "No!" and redirect it to an acceptable climbing spot. Repeat this step as many times as necessary.

❊ Be sure to put away all food when you are done cooking. Leaving goodies out where the cat can get to them will entice your pet to jump onto the counter. Also, if the item is made of chocolate or another ingredient toxic to cats, you could be looking at a trip to the emergency vet.

❊ Whenever you finish cooking, wipe counters with a citrus-scented cleaner. In addition to removing any crumbs that could summon the cat, the smell will act as a deterrent.

❊ If the cat still insists on making the counter part of its daily rounds, place sheets of aluminum foil across the surface. Your pet will find the sound that this item makes unpleasant and almost certainly jump down at once.

You create a distraction and I'll jump up and get them.

Okay, on the count of three: 1, 2 ...

DON'T TRY THIS AT HOME!

You may have heard that using mousetraps can help to keep cats off countertops. The theory behind this ill-advised strategy is that setting traps upside down or underneath sheets of newspaper on the counter will frighten the cat away if it should jump up onto this surface. While the idea of using noise as a deterrent is practical, the chance of injury is simply too high. There are many other ways of dealing with this common problem that will not maim a cat for life.

IF YOUR CAT TRACKS LITTER

Some cats can make quite a mess with their litter, enthusiastically scattering it around and tracking some of it with them when they step out of the box. Here are some tips for keeping the litter box area tidy:

❖ Purchase a litter box mat to catch the stray litter. If the mat you choose has a harsh surface, though, it may be counterproductive. Many cats will simply jump over a mat with a rough surface, scattering the mess even farther. So-called sticky mats work much better and can be wiped repeatedly to restore the tacky texture.

❖ Place a soft, washable throw rug in front of the litter box. While not as good as a mat at trapping the litter, a rug will not bother the cat's paws whatsoever. When you clean the litter box, vacuum the rug, and wash it as needed.

❖ Place the litter box inside a bigger litter box, so that the cat has to step into the larger box upon exiting the smaller one. Any litter that escapes the first box should be contained by the second. Some owners find that a shallow cardboard box works even better, especially for smaller cats and kittens.

❖ Invest in a top-entry litter box. A box that the cat enters and exits from the top reduces the amount of scattered litter significantly. Do hang onto the old litter box, though, until you are certain that your pet will use the new one. Some cats are fearful of covered boxes at first.

SHALLOW CAN BE GOOD

Most owners use far more litter in their cat's litter box than necessary. A cat can use a box filled with as little as ½ inch (13 mm) of litter or as much as 2 inches (5 cm). Any more than this amount is a waste and can make cleaning the cat's box more difficult than it has to be. By keeping the level of litter to a minimum, you can scoop out soiled matter and keep odor and mess to a minimum as well. You also save money and help ensure that the cat remains well trained. Cats are much more likely to use a clean, fresh litter box than a dirty, smelly one.

Up and Away!

Cats are remarkably athletic and can jump about five times their own height in a single leap.

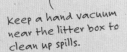

❖ A small amount of litter will inevitably escape the box, no matter what type of box or mat you use. Keep a small hand vacuum near the litter box and do a quick cleanup whenever you remove waste.

Keep a hand vacuum near the litter box to clean up spills.

A mother cat nursing her newborn kittens.

AVERAGE LITTER SIZE

First-time mothers usually give birth to two or three kittens. Cats that have had previous litters usually have more kittens, typically four or five.

Why Do Cats Knead?

❏ **They are territorial.**
❏ **They are happy.**
❏ **They are natural optimists.**

Answer: All of the above. Some cats knead as a means of marking their territory. Cats have scent glands in their paw pads that are released when they knead. Other cats knead to express contentment and emotional security. When a kitten wants to nurse, it uses its paws to knead its mother. This action stimulates the milk flow. Many cats continue this behavior into adulthood simply out of habit. Since the act produced a reward at one time, they may be hoping that it will do so again.

LARGEST LITTER
The largest litter of kittens ever delivered was by a Siamese cat. She had 19 kittens, but four of them were stillborn.

Oldest Feline Mother

The oldest known cat to give birth belonged to a man named George Johnstone of England. In May of 1987, Kitty was 30 years old when she delivered two kittens.

Cats have scent glands in their paw pads.

If cats and dogs are introduced to each other carefully, they can live together happily and peacefully.

Cats cannot taste sweetness.

SWEET NOTHINGS

Cats are the only mammals whose taste buds lack the ability to detect sweetness. Cats also cannot digest sugar, and feeding a cat sugar increases its chance of developing diabetes. Try to avoid cat foods that include ingredients like corn, which is a carbohydrate sweetener.

Teaching Tolerance

If you have both a cat and a dog, one of the most important things for you to teach your canine pet is the "Leave it" command. This simple instruction will come in handy if the dog ever decides that it might be fun to chase the cat. Although most dogs and cats can coexist peacefully together, some dogs need a little extra supervision and training in the beginning.

Some cats and dogs become the best of friends.

INTRODUCING A CAT TO ITS CARRIER

Most cats do not enjoy going for rides, but your feline companion should be able to tolerate a ride in its carrier when it needs to visit the veterinarian.

❶ Allow the cat some time to get used to the carrier before placing your pet inside it. Set it on the floor with the door open, allowing the cat to inspect it freely for at least a day or two if possible.

❷ Encourage the cat to go inside the carrier by placing one of its favorite edible treats inside. Some cats will walk into a carrier even without this type of enticement. If your pet enters the carrier, offer praise, but don't close the door.

❸ If the cat does not enter the carrier on its own, gently place your pet inside. Praise the cat for its compliance, but still don't close that door—yet.

❹ Once the cat has been inside the carrier a few times, start closing the door for short periods of time. If your pet protests by making lots of noise, try to wait for a small period of silence before opening the door. You do not want to teach the cat that screeching is the quickest way out.

❺ Finally, try placing the carrier inside your automobile.

WATER SUPPLY

Whenever traveling with a cat, be sure to take along plenty of fresh water. If a cat goes too long without drinking, it could suffer from dehydration. If the air temperature is high, lack of water also places a cat at an increased risk for heatstroke. It is the temperature inside the vehicle that matters. Even in the dead of winter, an automobile's heater can make the air as hot as it might be in the middle of summer. Most pet supply stores sell collapsible bowls that can be stored easily (in a glove compartment, for instance) when not in use. Some carriers come with a handy water bowl attachment.

Make the carrier more comfortable for your pet by lining it with a pad, blanket, or towel.

Portable water bowl

HOW OLD IS YOUR CAT?

You have probably heard the phrase "dog years," referring to
the theory that one year in a dog's life is comparable to seven
for a person. Did you know that there is a similar formula for
determining cat years? Once a cat reaches the age of two, each
additional year is thought to be equal to four human years.

Cats sometimes crunch dry food
to break it into smaller pieces.

EASY TO SWALLOW

* A cat does not need to chew its food. For humans to
swallow and properly digest food, we must grind it into
small pieces with our teeth first. As we chew, enzymes
from saliva help to break down the food. Cat saliva
contains no such enzymes. Wild cats use their teeth
primarily for killing prey and tearing the meat into
chunks that are just small enough to swallow whole.
Domestic cats have retained this ability.

* You may hear your pet crunch a piece of dry kibble
once or twice, just enough to break it into slightly smaller
pieces. Dental-health food formulas typically require more
chewing. In general, though, a cat can continue to eat even
if it loses all its teeth. This evolutionary trait does not mean
that you should not care for your pet's teeth, however.
Periodontal disease can lead to a number of other
dangerous health problems.

Cat Years	Human Years
1	15
2	24
3	28
4	32
5	36
6	40
7	44
8	48
9	52
10	56
11	60
12	64
13	68
14	72
15	76
16	80
17	84
18	88
19	92
20	96

"Meow" Translated

Meow is the most common sound that cats make, and it has many meanings. Similar to human infants, cats usually use different types of meows to express different feelings. Also similar to the parents of those newborn babies, cat owners can often discern what their pets are trying to tell them, either through the animal's tone or its body language. Sometimes, though, the meaning may not be clear. Interestingly, cats do not meow at other cats. This sound that we think of as being uniquely feline is actually reserved for interactions with people. Owners reinforce meowing when they respond to the sound by providing the cat with whatever it is seeking.

❖ **Friendly:** Short, high-pitched meows are friendly in nature.

❖ **Angry:** Longer meows typically mean that a cat is angry. Tone is important here. When a cat wants to sound intimidating, it lowers its pitch.

❖ **Pleading:** A pleading meow often begins with soft purring.

❖ **Alarm:** If a cat meows loudly in an unpleasant tone, it is trying to tell you that something is wrong. The louder and more distasteful the sound, the more dire the situation likely is.

ROYAL CATS OF SIAM

Members of the royal family of Siam used to be interred in a burial chamber that had small holes in the roof. A live cat would be buried with them. If the cat managed to escape, this was seen as a sign that the spirit of the buried person had passed into the cat.

The Siamese is the most vocal cat breed.

Me, a chatterbox? What a thing to say! I hardly ever say a word. Why, just the other day I was telling my friend...

A Savannah kitten, with the distinctive color markings, large ears, and long legs of its wild relative, the serval.

The serval uses its huge ears and acute hearing to detect the presence of rodents, both above and below ground.

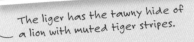

The liger has the tawny hide of a lion with muted tiger stripes.

HYBRID BREEDS

Hybrids are crosses between different breeds. There are three types:

* **Domestic/domestic hybrid:** The Himalayan is an example of a domestic/domestic hybrid. It is a cross between the Persian and the Siamese cat.

* **Domestic/wild hybrid:** The Savannah is an example of a domestic/wild hybrid. It is a cross between a domestic cat and the serval.

* **Wild/wild hybrid:** The liger and tiglon are examples of wild/wild hybrids. A liger is a cross between a male lion and a female tiger; a tiglon is a cross between a female lion and a male tiger.

Something Wicked This Way Comes

The association between cats and witches began during the Middle Ages in Europe. The cat came to be viewed as a sinister creature, linked with the devil. Its important role in pagan festivals, such as those of the Egyptian feline goddess Bastet, combined with the animal's independent and nocturnal habits, served to condemn it as a symbol of evil.

WITCH'S FAMILIAR

✤ In medieval times, many people believed that black cats were actually witches in disguise.

✤ Others believed that after seven years of service, a witch's feline companion would be rewarded by being transformed into a witch itself.

✤ These beliefs gave rise to the superstition that a black cat crossing your path brings bad luck, since the event was thought to be an encounter with a witch.

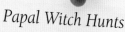

Papal Witch Hunts

★ Pope Gregory IX announced the link between black cats and the devil in the 10th century, and in 962 hundreds of cats were burned for their sins during Lent in the town of Metz, France.

★ During the 15th century, Pope Innocent VIII condemned the feline species, asserting that all cats were evil. As a result, thousands of cats were burned. One of the effects of this mass killing was an overpopulation of rats, which caused the Black Death to take an even greater toll on the human population.

Rat

A 17th-century woodcut of witches and their black cat familiars. For centuries, just owning a cat was considered incriminating evidence against anyone accused of witchcraft.

FUNNY BUT TRUE
"A black cat crossing your path signifies that the animal is going somewhere."
Groucho Marx

Oops

A Positive Approach

✿ Your cat is bound to make some mistakes during training. Whether your pet has jumped onto the counter or table, eliminated outside its litter box, or scratched a piece of furniture, never use physical punishment of any kind. Striking the cat can hurt it, and doing so will definitely hurt your relationship with your pet.

✿ When a cat behaves badly, offer a firm "No!" If the cat continues the unwanted behavior, consider using a spray bottle filled with water or clapping your hands to avert the action.

✿ More importantly, focus on praising the cat when you catch it doing something right. Actions that result in praise tend to be repeated.

ABRUPT CHANGES IN TEMPERAMENT

When a friendly cat suddenly turns aggressive or sullen, an illness may be the cause. A cat that is in pain may react negatively if it is disturbed while resting. If a cat's temperament has changed abruptly, look for signs of a health issue. Even if you cannot pinpoint a physical cause for the problem, a call to the veterinarian may be in order.

A GRAIN OF SALT

Cats are surrendered to shelters for numerous reasons. Sometimes volunteers know a lot about a particular cat's history; sometimes they know next to nothing. Many facilities ask surrendering owners to fill out a short questionnaire that asks about each animal's medical history, personality, and housetraining habits. This information can then be passed on to potential new owners. It is important that you do not rely too heavily on this information, however. Shelter volunteers have no way of knowing when a surrendering owner is being honest. Some surrendering owners may even refuse to fill out a questionnaire.

A change in temperament could indicate an illness.

Exhibition hall at the Catsburg international cat show in Moscow.

A judge at the Catsburg cat show assessing a Persian against its breed standard.

An Early Showing

★ The first cat show ever recorded was held in 1598 at St. Giles Fair in Winchester, England, but the first properly benched show, with cats being placed in individual cages, took place at London's Crystal Palace on July 13th, 1871. The show attracted 160 entrants, primarily featuring British Shorthairs and Persians. The first benched American cat show was held in Madison Square Garden, New York, in 1895.

★ Cats are assessed by qualified judges who relate each cat's qualities to its breed standard—an official written list of points describing what a particular breed should look like and how it should behave—and then rank each cat in order of merit. Non-pedigree domestic cats have a special section at most shows, and are judged on temperament, condition, and aesthetic appeal.

Cat Show Disqualifications

✦ Blindness
✦ Cosmetic surgery
✦ Crossed eyes
✦ Cut hair (except in allowed areas)
✦ Deafness (white cats okay)
✦ Declawing (primarily in Europe)
✦ Dyed hair
✦ Extra toes
✦ Misaligned skull bones
✦ Monorchidism (only one testicle descended) or cryptorchidism (neither testicle descended)
✦ No tail (Manx and Cymric okay)
✦ Protruding or misaligned jaw
✦ Short tail (bobtail breeds okay)
✦ Signs of aggression
✦ Signs of pregnancy
✦ Any other trait deemed unacceptable by the breed standard

LAP-SITTERS

- Birman
- Bombay
- Burmese
- Chartreux
- Cornish Rex
- Devon Rex
- Havana Brown
- LaPerm
- Nebelung
- Ocicat
- Oriental Shorthair
- Persian
- Ragdoll
- Russian Blue
- Scottish Fold
- Selkirk Rex
- Siamese
- Sphynx

The Burmese is sometimes called the "Velcro cat" because it loves to be around people.

Burmese and Tonkinese

✱ Burmese cats are surprisingly heavy for their size. On the outside, these gorgeous creatures are blue, champagne, platinum, or sable—but on the inside they are all muscle. They are often referred to as bricks wrapped in silk.

✱ All modern Burmese cats can trace their ancestry back to a female named Wong Mau, who was taken from Rangoon to the United States in 1930. Wong Mau was almost certainly a cat of the type known as Tonkinese today.

✱ Once known as the Golden Siamese, the Tonkinese is a hybrid of Burmese and Siamese cats. A mating between a Burmese and a Siamese produces all Tonkinese kittens, whereas the mating of two Tonkinese cats produces, on average, two Tonkinese kittens to one Burmese and one Siamese.

Although not a lap-sitter, the Tonkinese is known for enjoying sitting on its owner's shoulders.

QUESTIONS TO ASK A PET SITTER

- Are you bonded and insured?
- Do you have references?
- Which veterinarian do you use if an animal gets sick or becomes injured?
- Do you work with another pet sitter who can serve as a backup if needed?
- Do you charge per pet, per visit, or a flat fee?
- Do you own cats yourself?

ASSESSING THE ANSWERS

The exact answers to these questions are less important than your comfort level with the potential pet sitter and his or her responses. Most pet owners prefer that a sitter be bonded and insured. References are also important to many people, although sitters are unlikely to give you the names and contact information of people who are apt to give them bad reviews. If you want the sitter to use your veterinarian in the event of a medical problem, make this clear. You may also want to inform the veterinarian that this person will be caring for your pet—and has your permission to make decisions on your behalf while you are gone. Whether the sitter is a cat owner should not be a deal breaker, but the question usually opens the door for a conversation about how the person feels about cats and animals in general. So-called dog people can make excellent caregivers for cats, but anyone who dislikes or fears cats is usually not the best choice.

Call It Karma

"People who hate cats will come back as mice in their next life."
Faith Resnick

Pop Feline

* In the 1950s, Andy Warhol published a book of cat portraits entitled *25 Cats Name Sam and One Blue Pussy*. The book featured lithographs of 16 cats, each named Sam, and one cat captioned "One Blue Pussy."

* Warhol's mother contributed the calligraphy in the book. She omitted the final "d" from "Name" in the title, but Warhol liked the error and kept it.

* Warhol and his mother were great cat lovers, and had several cats named Sam and one cat named Hester. However, the portraits in the book were based on the work of cat photographer Walter Chandoha, not on Warhol's own cats.

* Warhol gave most of the limited edition, privately printed books as gifts to friends and clients.

Andy Warhol

Is your cat a social networker?

TECHNO-KITTY

Cats have joined the electronic age.

✤ Did you know that you can download iPad games specifically for your cat? One such program features a digital mouse that darts across the screen, virtually begging to be chased.

✤ The Nintendo game Wii Fit Plus allows pet owners to create avatars for their cats and keep track of their weight and fitness routines right along with their own.

✤ There is even a Facebook application called Catbook, where you can upload photos of your pet and "friend" other felines.

Cat Traps

Open drawers can be an accident waiting to happen. If a cat climbs into one and falls asleep when you are not looking, you could trap your pet when you close the drawer. Even worse, the cat could climb over the back of the drawer to the empty space behind it. This maneuver could result in your pet being injured when you close the drawer.

Open drawers are enticing to a cat, and your pet could get trapped inside.

DANGEROUS PLACES WHERE CATS CAN GET TRAPPED

- Kitchen or bathroom cupboards
- Ovens
- Refrigerators and freezers
- Washing machines and dryers

PUT A LID ON IT

One of the easiest things you can do to keep a curious kitty out of trouble is to purchase wastebaskets with covers for your home. For the sake of your own convenience, look for models that offer a step-on lever to open and close them. Remember to use covered wastebaskets in both kitchens and bathrooms. Many of the items that have the greatest potential for harming your pet— things like dental floss and disposable razors—are thrown away in the bathroom.

When to Lower the Lid

If your cat drinks water from the toilet, it is very important that you keep the lid closed at all times. Even trace amounts of the chemical products used for cleaning toilets can make your pet sick.

A Scottish wildcat hunting for prey.

Hemingway

USA 25

Wildcats: The Closest Cousin

❂ The wildcat (*Felis sylvestris*) has one of the most extensive ranges of all the non-domestic species of cat, ranging from northern parts of Europe down to the tip of southern Africa, and eastward through the Middle East into Asia.

❂ Within its range, several subspecies have been identified, with the African population (*F. s. lybica*) being the ancestor of the domestic cat. African wildcats are generally less aggressive than European wildcats.

❂ The wildcat's relatively small size and shy nature, plus the fact that it poses no direct threat to humans, allow it to live undisturbed, at least where it poses no threat to farm animals.

❂ Ironically, the greatest threat to the wildcat today, especially across Europe, is its ability to mate with the domestic cat because they are so closely related. In particular, male domestic cats often mate with female wildcats, producing hybridized offspring.

PET-QUALITY PUREBREDS

If you like the look of a particular breed but cannot afford the expensive price tag of a show-quality animal, ask the breeder about purchasing a pet-quality kitten. A pet-quality cat can make an excellent companion. It simply falls short of matching the breed standard closely enough to compete in cat shows.

CHINESE CATS

✽ Cats reached China around 400 C.E., and in 595 an empress was recorded as having been bewitched by a cat spirit.

✽ By the 12th century, rich Chinese families kept yellow and white cats known as "lion cats," which were highly valued as pets.

✽ The Chinese god of agriculture, Li Shou, took the form of a cat and was worshipped by peasant farmers, who made sacrifices to him at the end of the harvest.

CAT TALES

One old folk belief states that cutting off hairs from a cat's tail and burying them under the doorstep keeps a cat from roaming.

Viking

A young Norwegian Forest Cat

Feline Explorers

Norwegian Forest Cats appear in Norse myths and fairy stories. The cats are also said to have sailed the world with Vikings. In exchange for their fare, the cats protected the ships' food stores from vermin.

A kitten with the distinctive "M" marking on its forehead that is common to tabbies.

Cat in the Manger

A folktale about the Christian nativity tells of how there was a cat in the stable giving birth to a litter of kittens at the same time that Mary was giving birth to Jesus. When the newborn baby would not sleep, Mary asked all the animals in the stable if they could help, but none was able to get the child to sleep. Finally, a little gray tabby kitten climbed into the manger and curled up next to Jesus, who fell asleep to the gentle sound of its purring. Mary rewarded the kitten by allowing all tabby cats from that time forth to wear a letter "M" (for Madonna) on their foreheads. This charming tale has influenced many artists, most notably Leonardo da Vinci, who included a cat and kittens as a part of many of his studies of the Madonna and child.

Madonna and child

CARPET CLEANING WOES

✛ *Before shampooing a carpet, check to see if the cleaning agent is safe to use around pets. Cats lick their paws and bodies to clean them, so any chemicals that your pet encounters can end up in its digestive system and make it sick. In some cases, the effects can be deadly. When buying a cleaning product, look for one that is labeled "nontoxic" or "safe to use around pets."*

✛ *The best cleaners are the ones made from natural ingredients. Everyday products that are probably sitting on the shelves of your kitchen pantry right now can be remarkably good at cleaning carpets and other household items. Baking soda, vinegar, and club soda are all excellent at removing stains as well as odors.*

LACTOSE INTOLERANCE

Although your cat may enjoy drinking a saucer of milk or cream, many cats have bad reactions to consuming these and other dairy products. Like some people, cats lack the digestive enzyme needed to break down lactose in the stomach. The effects of feeding dairy to a cat can range from mild diarrhea to severe abdominal pain. Some cats can tolerate small amounts of milk or cream if they are diluted with a little water and offered only occasionally.

Some cats like milk as a treat, but it is best avoided.

KEEPING KITTY HYDRATED

A cat needs to drink about 1 ounce (30 ml) of water per pound (450 g) of body weight each day. Cats that eat wet food will fulfill a portion of their daily water requirement through eating alone. Cats on dry diets need to drink more. A healthy cat will drink what it needs, but if you do have concerns about your cat's level of hydration, here are some tips to help you entice your pet to drink more water:

✤ **Keep it clean.** Cats like drinking fresh water from clean dishes. Many will refuse to drink from a bowl that has been topped off or refilled. If the cat's water dish is made of plastic, replace it with a stainless steel bowl. Plastic is notorious for trapping odors, and using a basin with lingering odors is a surefire way to discourage a cat from drinking the water.

✤ **Try a new location.** As strange as it may sound, many cats dislike drinking from a water dish that is right next to a food dish. If a cat is not drinking much, try moving its water bowl to another location. Just be sure to direct the cat to the new spot when you relocate it.

✤ **Filter the water.** If the cat dislikes your tap water, consider investing in a water filtration system to make the water taste better. These systems are more cost effective and environmentally friendly than buying bottled water.

✤ **Check the temperature.** Many cats have an aversion to eating or drinking anything cold. If you use bottled water, don't refrigerate the cat's portion. If the water from the tap is too cold, fill the cat's water bowl and allow it to reach room temperature before serving it. Don't allow the water to sit so long that it becomes stagnant, though.

✤ **Buy a pet fountain.** If the cat only enjoys drinking its water immediately after it is served, perhaps a pet fountain could bring your pet back for more. Many cats are attracted to the moving water of a fountain, so they are more likely to drink from one than from their conventional bowls.

A healthy cat will stay hydrated as long as it has access to plenty of fresh drinking water.

The dainty little Korat is alert, inquisitive, and affectionate.

ACTIVE BREEDS

- ✦ Abyssinian
- ✦ American Curl
- ✦ Balinese
- ✦ Bengal
- ✦ Birman
- ✦ Burmese
- ✦ Colorpoint Shorthair
- ✦ Cornish Rex
- ✦ Devon Rex
- ✦ Egyptian Mau
- ✦ Japanese Bobtail
- ✦ Javanese
- ✦ Korat
- ✦ LaPerm
- ✦ Ocicat
- ✦ Oriental Shorthair
- ✦ Siamese
- ✦ Siberian
- ✦ Singapura
- ✦ Somali
- ✦ Sphynx
- ✦ Tonkinese
- ✦ Turkish Angora
- ✦ Turkish Van

Good Fortune

★ In its native Thailand, the Korat is known as the Si-Sawat, which means good luck. Pairs of these cats are often given to brides in Thailand to ensure good fortune in their marriage.

★ The *Cat Book Poems*, written in Thailand between 1350 and 1767, includes illustrations and lyrical descriptions of different breeds of cat. It says of the Korat: "The cat Mal-ed has a body like Doklao. The hairs are smooth with roots like clouds and tips like silver. The eyes shine like dewdrops on a lotus leaf." "Mal-ed" refers to the seed of the "look sawat," a silvery gray fruit lightly tinged with green. "Dok" is a flower, and "lao" a plant with silver-tipped flowers.

Devil May Care

The Somali is the longhaired version of the Abyssinian. The breed is known for its intense energy level and keen intelligence. These cats typically zoom through their homes several times a day, chasing toys or jumping through the air. Somalis are extremely adept at opening cabinet doors and drawers, and can even learn to turn on water faucets.

The Somali makes a playful and athletic pet.

HALLOWEEN HORRORS

Even if you normally allow your cat to roam freely outdoors, you may want to keep it inside around Halloween. Although much of the hype surrounding cat sacrifices by satanic cults is just that—hype—black cats in particular can be common targets for mistreatment around this time of year. Many shelters put a moratorium on adoptions around Halloween to prevent their animals from becoming victims of abuse. When it comes to a cat's well-being, it is far better to be safe than sorry.

BIGGEST AND SMALLEST CAT BREEDS

- The Maine Coon and the Ragdoll are generally considered to be the largest fully domestic cat breeds, with males weighing as much as 20 pounds (9 kg). Some wild/domestic hybrid breeds are larger.
- The Guinness Book of World Records lists the Singapura as the world's smallest domestic cat breed. Males can weigh as little as 6 pounds (270 g); females can weigh just 4 pounds (180 g).

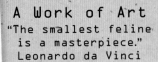

A Work of Art
"The smallest feline is a masterpiece."
Leonardo da Vinci

Singapura

In its native Singapore, this breed was once referred to as the Drain Cat, because the city's street cats (from which the breed appears to have originated) used to seek shelter in the large, open monsoon drains during the dry season. This lifestyle is a probable cause of their smaller bodies, in comparison with other oriental breeds. The Singapura is a happy, friendly cat, and its street ancestry has equipped the animal to adapt quickly and easily to whatever situation it finds itself in.

In the 1990s, the Singapura was used as a tourism mascot for Singapore under the name "Kucinta, the Love Cat of Singapore."

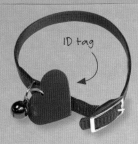

ID tag

KEEP IT SIMPLE

✤ *If you want a cat to learn its name, keep it short and simple. Choose a name no longer than one or two syllables.*

✤ *You may want to select several names and try each one out. Say the name in an upbeat tone. If the cat responds by looking up when you say a certain name, it may just be the best one for your pet.*

✤ *Avoid calling the cat by nicknames, because this will make things confusing.*

✤ *While the cat is learning its name, be prepared to dispense a reward whenever you call your pet. The reward does not have to be edible. Praise will work just fine, although a treat or two certainly will not hurt.*

✤ *Never use the cat's name when something even mildly unpleasant is about to happen—such as a bath or a trip to the veterinarian—or you may inadvertently create a bad connotation for your pet to its own name.*

MICROCHIPS AND ID TAGS

If your cat goes missing, the best thing you could have done to increase the chances of finding your pet is to have provided it with a reliable form of identification.

☆ The best form of pet identification is a microchip. This tiny device can literally save the cat's life if your pet should go missing. The vet inserts the microchip, which is about the size of a grain of rice, under the cat's skin, typically between the shoulder blades. The procedure is as quick and virtually painless as a vaccination.

☆ Placing an ID tag on the cat's collar is also a smart safety precaution, but bear in mind that collars can slip off surprisingly easily sometimes. Other times they have help. People known as bunchers make a living by selling pets to dealers who sell animals to laboratories. The biggest advantage of a microchip is that it is not going anywhere. Even tattoos, the most common form of permanent identification in years past, can be altered by a resourceful criminal.

☆ Most shelters and veterinary hospitals are equipped with scanners that help them to identify lost pets that have been microchipped. Owners must register the cat's chip with the appropriate company and update their contact information if it changes. The number of the cat's microchip can only help reunite the two of you if the company knows how to reach you.

A microchip injection is quick and virtually painless.

Feeding Through the Ages

Age	What to Feed	How Much	How Often	Special Instructions
Young kittens (12 weeks to 6 months)	Keep the kitten on the same food that its breeder fed it until the kitten has acclimated to your home. If you wish to change to a different food, do so gradually to avoid digestive upset.	Follow the breeder's instructions regarding quantities when you first take the kitten home. The kitten will begin eating more as it continues to grow.	Feed 5 to 6 meals a day.	Kittens need to eat more frequently than older cats due to their tiny stomach and faster metabolism.
Kittens (6 months to 1 year)	Choose a high-quality food made specifically for young cats. Kitten formulas have more calories and higher amounts of protein, amino acids, and minerals than adult food.	Follow package directions, but a general rule is one-third of a cup per day.	Feed 3 times a day.	If the kitten is not eating enough, soak its food in milk replacer or warm water to make it more appealing.

2-month-old Persian

7-month-old British Shorthair

5-year-old Siamese

12-year-old Persian

On Feeding

"I have noticed that what cats most appreciate in a human being is not the ability to produce food which they take for granted—but his or her entertainment value."
Geoffrey Household

Age	What to Feed	How Much	How Often	Special Instructions
Adults (Between 1 and 10 years)	If the cat fared well eating a particular food as a kitten, it may be smart to continue with the same brand in an adult formula once the cat reaches its full size.	Follow package directions based on the cat's weight and activity level. An 8-pound (3.6-kg) Oriental Shorthair needs fewer calories than a 16-pound (7.2-kg) Maine Coon. Likewise, an active cat needs more calories than a couch potato.	Feed 2 or 3 times a day.	Changes may be necessary from time to time. If the cat becomes overweight, a diet formula may be necessary. Likewise, cats that are prone to urinary infections should eat wet food instead of dry.
Seniors (10 years and upward)	As the cat gets older, its metabolism will slow down. To prevent unnecessary weight gain, swap your pet to a senior formula at this time.	Follow package directions, but also watch your pet's weight. This is the best way of assessing whether the cat is eating enough but not too much.	Aging cats can develop especially finicky appetites. For this reason, it may be wise to feed a senior cat several smaller meals throughout the day, rather than 2 or 3 larger ones.	You can help prevent a slowing metabolism from hurting your pet's health by making regular exercise a continued priority.

A Persian cat from New Delhi, India, may be the world's smartest feline. His owner, Hema Mohan Chandra, claims that Cuty Boy can solve complicated math problems and understand questions posed to him in eight languages. The cat answers by bumping his owner with his nose a certain number of times. Critics insist that the cat is merely responding to cues that his owner is unconsciously providing. While they agree that his abilities are remarkable, they consider them to be more about perception than mathematical knowledge.

INTELLIGENT BREEDS

- Abyssinian
- American Bobtail
- Balinese
- Bengal
- Bombay
- Burmese
- Chartreux
- Colorpoint Shorthair
- Devon Rex
- Egyptian Mau
- Havana Brown
- Javanese
- Korat
- Manx
- Norwegian Forest Cat
- Ocicat
- Oriental Shorthair
- Russian Blue
- Siamese
- Siberian
- Singapura
- Somali
- Sphynx
- Tonkinese
- Turkish Angora
- Turkish Van

An Egyptian sphinx, guardian of temples and tombs.

The Mythical Sphinx

The mythical sphinx has a lion's body and a human head. It has been depicted in different cultures around the world since ancient times, sometimes as a benevolent creature and sometimes malevolent.

THE HAIRLESS SPHYNX

The Sphynx cat breed is best known for being virtually hairless due to a recessive mutation. It comes in all the same colors and patterns as other breeds do, since coat color in cats is literally more than skin deep. The Sphynx originated in Toronto, Canada, in 1966. This breed is a practical option for many cat lovers who are allergic to cat hair. As you may imagine, Sphynxes get cold more easily than other cats, so owners must be mindful of temperature. Sphynxes also get dirty more quickly than other breeds. Use a baby wipe with lanolin to give your Sphynx a sponge bath in between conventional baths.

Outdoor Exposure

Indoor cats can enjoy time outside, provided their owners take a few precautions. Regular outdoor time can lessen boredom, reduce stress, and even help with litter box and other behavior problems. Here are some great ideas for giving a feline friend some fresh air:

* Take the cat outdoors on a harness and leash.

* Build an outdoor enclosure with lumber and chicken wire, or buy one.

* Invest in an invisible containment system. This consists of a transmitter and a cat collar with an electronic receiver. If the cat wearing the collar approaches the established boundary, the transmitter sends a signal to the collar and the cat receives a warning. It is essential that the cat be properly trained if the system is to be effective; systems come with training advice.

* If you have a fenced yard, you can add a cat fence topper. This involves attaching poles to the top of the existing fence. The poles project inward over the garden and support a mesh material that acts as a physical barrier between the cat and the world outside the safety of the yard. In order for the topper to attach and work correctly, the fence must be strong, tall, and constructed of either chain link or wood. Remember also that even the best fence topper will not prevent a crafty cat from escaping through a weak area in the fence itself, or through a gap between the fence and the ground.

A Sphynx being taken for a walk on a harness and leash, wearing a coat to protect its hairless body from the elements.

Single or Double

Most cats have two layers of fur—a topcoat and an undercoat. Cats lacking an undercoat tend to shed the least, whereas those with profuse undercoats usually shed the most.

WHY DO CATS SHED?

✤ Animals shed as a means of ridding their coats of dead hair and making room for new hair growth. Cats that spend a lot of time outdoors build up heavier coats in the winter and shed more during the spring. Indoor cats tend to shed more consistently all year long.

✤ All cats shed, but certain breeds shed more than others, and shorthaired cats often shed just as much as their furrier counterparts. The Maine Coon, Persian, and Somali breeds are prolific shedders. The Burmese, Siamese, and Tonkinese breeds are known for shedding far less than other cats.

✤ Owners can minimize shedding by taking a few simple steps. Regular brushing is one of the best ways to remove excess hair from the cat's coat. Brushing also removes dirt and other debris—and feels pretty good, too, for both pet and owner.

✤ What you choose to feed a cat can influence how much your pet sheds. Cats that eat high-quality food rich in omega-3 and omega-6 fatty acids are less prone to excessive shedding. They also have fewer skin problems.

✤ When you cannot reduce shedding, you can limit the effect it has on your household and the people in it. Provide your pet with plenty of furniture. Comfy cat beds and carpeted cat trees make great places for your feline friend to relax and play.

USE A TOWEL

If the cat spends a lot of time on furniture, place blankets or towels in its favorite spots during peak shedding periods. You can remove these impromptu furniture covers whenever company arrives.

MALES VERSUS FEMALES

Which is better—a male or female cat? Some owners insist that male cats are more affectionate than females. Others prefer females, because they are usually smaller and less prone to unpleasant behaviors such as urine marking. Neutering reduces this tendency significantly. As long as you have the cat sterilized, you should not notice a huge difference between the two sexes.

Boy or girl? Can you tell the difference?

Sculpture of a cat in La Romieu, France.

Cat Grass

If your cat spends time outdoors, you may notice that it enjoys chewing on fresh grass. Many owners do not realize that indoor cats can also enjoy this vitamin-rich, high-fiber treat. Cat grass grows quickly and is low maintenance, making it a practical renewable resource. Simply sow some seeds in one or more nonbreakable pots, and soon your pet will have its own indoor garden. Providing a cat with its own edible grass is also the best way to keep it from snacking on household plants. Safe grasses for a cat include:

❁ Barley
❁ Catmint
❁ Catnip
❁ Chickweed
❁ Lawn grass
❁ Oat

❁ Parsley
❁ Rye
❁ Sage
❁ Thyme
❁ Wheat grass

Village of the Cats

La Romieu in southwestern France is known as the "Village of the Cats." The story goes that in the 14th century, after a terrible harvest and harsh winter, it was decided that the starving villagers should eat all of the village cats in order to survive. A young girl named Angeline spared the lives of one male and one female cat, and looked after them in secret. Although the following year's crop flourished, the harvest was threatened because the fields were overrun with rodents. Luckily, Angeline's cats had had several litters of kittens by then, and she was able to release her feline friends to save the harvest and the village from ruin.

Feline Fables and Fairy Tales

Feline characters have featured in numerous fables, fairy tales, and children's stories. Here are some of examples:

RÉPUBLIQUE FRANÇAISE · LA POSTE 1997 · EUROPA · 3,00 · PERRAULT · LE CHAT BOTTÉ

Stamp featuring an engraving of Puss in Boots by Gustave Doré.

FELINE FABULISTS

❖ Among the earliest written works to include cats were Aesop's fables, a series of stories attributed to a Greek slave and storyteller named Aesop living around the 6th century B.C.E. The stories generally depict cats as crafty and dishonest.

❖ In the 17th century, French author Jean de la Fontaine wrote fables featuring a cat called Raminagrobis. The cat was wily and devious. In one fable, *The Cat, the Weasel, and the Rabbit*, the cat is asked to settle a quarrel between the other two characters. Pretending to be old and deaf, Raminagrobis asks them to come close so that he can hear their argument clearly. When they move nearer, he kills and eats them both.

DICK WHITTINGTON AND HIS CAT

The fairy tale of Dick Whittington became popular in the 17th century. It is the story of an orphaned English boy who travels from a country village to London, where the streets are said to be paved with gold. After enduring hardship, Dick gets a job in a kitchen and acquires a cat to help keep his room free of rodents. The cat's prowess at rat-catching eventually earns Dick his fortune, and he becomes Lord Mayor of London. The story is based on a real Lord Mayor by the name of Sir Richard Whittington (c.1354–1423), but he was never poor and unfortunately there is no evidence that he ever had a cat.

PUSS IN BOOTS

French author Charles Perrault wrote *The Master Cat*, or *Puss in Boots*, at the end of the 17th century. Based on a traditional folk tale, *Puss in Boots* is an example of a clever cat that brings luck to his owner. In the story, a miller's son receives a cat as his only inheritance. The cat promises to bring riches to the young man in return for a bag and a pair of boots. The resourceful cat uses his guile to secure a marriage between his owner and a princess, and goes on to enjoy a life of luxury himself.

Jean de la Fontaine

The Cheshire Cat could disappear gradually until only its grin remained.

THE CHESHIRE CAT

One of the most popular feline characters of all time is the Cheshire Cat from Lewis Carroll's classic children's book *Alice's Adventures in Wonderland*, first published in 1865. The character is so well known that a person with an especially mischievous grin on his or her face is often said to be "smiling like the Cheshire Cat."

THEODOR SEUSS GEISEL

THE CAT IN THE HAT

Written in simple rhyme, Dr. Seuss' best-known book *The Cat in the Hat* has been a children's favorite since 1957. It tells the story of a mischievous feline that visits a boy and girl one rainy day—and wreaks havoc on their entire home. At the same time, he teaches them how to enjoy life. The character was brought to the big screen in 2003 in the movie of the same name starring Mike Myers.

THE CATS OF HARRY POTTER

✣ Professor McGonagall, who teaches transfiguration, can change herself into a cat at will. Her feline counterpart is portrayed on screen by a silver tabby.

✣ Hermione Granger's pet cat and magical familiar, Crookshanks, is half domestic longhair and half Kneazle—a catlike creature that can detect the presence of untrustworthy beings. Crookshanks is played on screen by a red Persian.

✣ Mrs. Norris is caretaker Argus Filch's beloved yet unkempt cat. She roams the halls of Hogwarts with the ill-tempered caretaker. In the movies, Mrs. Norris is played by three different Maine Coon cats. Her trademark disheveled look was made possible by a collar of fake fur and nontoxic hair gel.

✣ Many scenes from the movies were filmed in drafty castles, so heated floors were installed specifically to keep the cats' paws and bodies warm.

✣ At one time, hairballs were believed to possess magical qualities. In *Harry Potter and the Half-blood Prince* (2005), Harry saves Ron's life with a cat's hairball when Ron accidentally drinks poisoned mead (honey wine).

КЫРГЫЗСТАН

50c KYRGRZSTAN

It's a Myth

It is a myth that if you bathe a cat it will never wash itself again. This old wives' tale likely began because most cats will not clean themselves if their coats become covered with an extremely foul-tasting substance, such as diesel oil. Although a cat may dislike the taste of soap, a little shampoo residue will not be enough to keep it from grooming itself.

Do not be fooled by my calm exterior. I will have my revenge...

Some cats will tolerate being rinsed using a shower spray, but try to keep the water off your pet's face.

DRY SHAMPOO

✣ Since many cats dislike water, giving your pet an occasional bath with dry shampoo is a great way to keep its coat clean and healthy without upsetting your feline friend. You can buy dry shampoo at a pet supply store, but make sure that the product you choose is formulated specifically for cats. Cats spend a great deal of time self-grooming by licking their fur. Any product that you apply to your pet's coat will be ingested to some degree.

✣ You can use bran or oatmeal as a natural dry shampoo. Warm it in an oven beforehand and rub it thoroughly into the cat's coat. This will prove a rather messy operation and is best carried out on newspaper outside. Groom the cat's coat afterward.

✣ Other effective dry shampoos are talcum powder and cornstarch. These should be sprinkled on the coat, rubbed in well, and then brushed out. Finish with grooming.

CAT HATERS

The following people are said to have detested cats:
- Napoleon Bonaparte
- Adolf Hitler
- Genghis Khan
- Benito Mussolini

Napoleon

It's Not the Fur

Many people think that cat allergies are caused by cat hair, but usually it is cat dander that causes the problem. The outer layer of a cat's skin, called the epidermis, is constantly renewing itself. As new layers push to the top surface of the skin, the old layers are shed. These dead layers flake off as dander. Even shorthaired and hairless cats produce dander.

BLAME IT ON TESTOSTERONE

Scientists have discovered that intact male cats produce more allergenic secretions through their skin than either neutered males or females.

HYPOALLERGENIC BREEDS— THE BEST BETS FOR ALLERGY SUFFERERS

• Balinese
• Cornish Rex
• Devon Rex
• Javanese
• Oriental Shorthair
• Siberian
• Sphynx

"Hypo" means low, so if you have an intense cat allergy, even a hypoallergenic breed may not be an option for you. Between 2 and 15 percent of people are allergic to cats. About a third of them are still able to live with a cat.

Kremlin Kat
The Siberian is the national cat of Russia.

The Siberian is thought to be the ancestor of all modern longhaired cat breeds.

Some cats have whiskers for eyebrows.

DEEP FEELINGS

A cat typically has 12 whiskers on each side of its nose. These long hairs, which are called vibrissae, are embedded deeper than the animal's other hairs. This depth is part of what makes the whiskers so sensitive to stimuli.

No Joke

Although they will regrow, you should never trim a cat's whiskers. Without its whiskers to help it judge the width of narrow spaces, a cat can get stuck in tight spots very easily.

ANOTHER REASON TO QUIT

If you smoke, you are increasing your cat's risk of developing several types of cancer.

✳ Squamous cell carcinoma, an oral cancer, is more common in cats whose owners light up. This elevated risk is likely linked to the cat's grooming habits. When cats lick their fur, they ingest toxins from secondhand smoke that have settled onto their coats.

✳ Cats with smoking owners also have higher rates of feline lymphoma than other cats as a result of inhaling secondhand smoke.

The Nighttime Naughties

Being active at night is as natural to a cat as stalking a mouse or cleaning its paws. Sometimes cats take this natural tendency too far, though.

✳ Some cats want to dart around the house and play when everyone else in the household is sleeping. Some cats even wake human family members by jumping on them in their beds—or meowing at bedroom doors if they are closed. Even the most beloved cat can seem like a nocturnal nightmare at these times.

✳ Trying to convince a cat to quiet down at your bedtime can be difficult, but it is not impossible. The secret is to indulge your pet before it is time for you to call it a night. Play with the cat, ideally once in the early evening and again shortly before you turn in. Before changing into pajamas, though, offer the cat a small amount of food. You can set aside a portion of its evening meal for this purpose.

✳ By simulating the act of hunting through play and substituting cat food for the captured prey, you just might satisfy the cat's nighttime urges so that everyone can get a good night's rest. When you see the cat licking its paws after its late-night snack, you will know that your pet is ready to call it a night, because this is how a wild cat readies itself for slumber after a successful nighttime hunt.

QUARANTINE

If you already have pets, you should establish a quarantine period when adding a new cat to the household.

❖ Keep the new cat in a separate room, away from the other pets, for about 10 days in case the new arrival has any infections that could spread. Schedule an appointment with a veterinarian as soon as possible to help rule out any health issues.

❖ The new cat will feel more secure in a smaller space initially. Provide plenty of food and water, a clean litter box, a warm place to sleep, and a toy or two. Although other animals should be kept away, it is important that you spend a good amount of time with the new arrival.

❖ When it is time to introduce the cat to the rest of the household, take it slowly and be patient. It can take up to a month for everyone to become comfortable with one another.

play with your cat before bedtime to satisfy its nighttime urge to hunt.

The Persecution of Cats

In medieval times when cats were associated with witchcraft, the animals suffered many forms of torture for public entertainment.

Louis XIV

Cat Throwing

In the town of Ypres in Belgium, there was a tradition of throwing cats from the top of the Cloth Tower in the town square. Starting as early as the 12th century, this activity continued until 1817 when it was finally outlawed. Originally, only one or two cats were thrown, but it became the practice to throw two cats in a bad year and three cats in a good year. The practice was resumed in 1938, when velvet cats were thrown instead of live ones. The festival, Kattenstoet, is now a tourist attraction held in May once every three years. It includes a parade, dressing up as cats, and the appointment of a cat queen, as well as the throwing of velvet and fabric cats from the tower.

Cat decoration at a window in Ypres, Belgium, for the Kattenstoet festival.

CAT BURNING

In France, the festival of St. John was celebrated annually in June with the burning alive of cats in town squares. The Celts had held a midsummer fire festival at which sacred animals were burned as sacrifices. The Christians superimposed St. John's Day on this festival, and perpetuated the practice of burning animals—this time cats, as creatures not of veneration but of evil. One of the greatest followers of this practice was King Louis XIV of France. Reference to this custom is made in a surviving receipt from a Lucas Pommérieux for money paid to him for "furnishing for a period of years, ending with the feast of St. John 1573, all the cats collected for the usual bonfire, and also for furnishing the large jute bags to carry the aforesaid cats."

THE INFAMOUS CAT ORGAN

The cat organ was a keyboard that, instead of operating pipes or hammers like a traditional organ or piano, pulled the tails of cats that were trapped in cages. The tails were pulled hard enough to encourage the cat to emit a loud sound, to the apparent amusement of onlookers. It was customary to release the cats from the organ eventually, so that they could be used for target practice by archers.

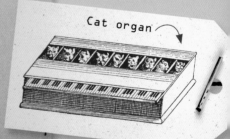

Cat organ

During the festival of St. John in France, cats used to be suspended above bonfires. In some places, fireworks were thrown into the fire along with the cats.

Scratch That

Scratching is instinctive behavior for cats; they do it to sharpen their claws and to mark out their territory. A cat is more likely to scratch the furniture if it does not go out or if there is another cat in the house. Luckily, there are a number of measures that you can use to deter a cat from discovering the delights of scratching your furniture.

* Be sure to provide a cat with plenty of acceptable outlets for its natural desire to scratch. Scratching posts are available in a wide array of designs, materials, and price ranges. Be sure that the post you choose is stable and tall enough for the cat to use while stretching its body completely—at least 28 inches (70 cm).

* If you catch the cat scratching an unacceptable item, offer a firm "No!" before redirecting your pet to a scratching post. Praise the cat for its compliance.

* Trim the cat's claws regularly. Many cats scratch much less often if their claws are kept short. Ask a veterinarian to show you how to cut them.

* Scratching deterrents are available at most pet supply stores. Sticky pads or strips can be an especially effective option. Since cats dislike the smell of citrus, lemon- or orange-scented sprays also work well. Be careful not to overuse them, though. You want to keep the cat away from whatever item it wants to sink its claws into, not an entire room.

* If a cat is insistent on scratching curtains, furniture, and other belongings, consider purchasing vinyl caps for your pet's claws. These rounded covers prevent the cat from doing damage through scratching and are a more humane alternative to declawing.

Scratching posts can range from simple and inexpensive models to elaborate and pricey towers that include hideouts and lookouts.

WHAT DOES DECLAWING ENTAIL?

Declawing is a surgical procedure to remove a cat's claws, usually carried out to prevent destructive scratching. It has been condemned by numerous cat organizations, and for good reason. The operation involves amputating the cat's nails and nail base, including the ends of the cat's toes right up to the first joint. Declawing for non-medical reasons is uncommon outside North America, and is illegal in many countries around the world, including Britain and Australia.

THE BEST DEFENSE

Never allow a declawed cat to roam freely outdoors. A cat's claws are its best defense against dogs, larger cats, and wild predators. Without its claws, a cat will not even be able to escape its pursuer by climbing a tree.

DO-IT-YOURSELF
SCRATCHING POSTS

Making a scratching post does not require many materials or any special skills.

❶ All you need is a log (including its bark), a wooden plank, and a small carpet remnant. Be sure to use wood that is safe for cats; check with a veterinarian if you are unsure.

❷ Begin by covering the plank with the carpet, pile side down, to ensure that the surface is rough enough. Nail the log onto the top of the carpeted plank by hammering the nails through from the bottom of the plank.

❸ If the cat becomes bored with the post after a while, wrap the log with some sisal carpet or burlap for a new texture.

Don't Toss It!

If your cat's scratching post is looking kind of worn and ugly, resist the urge to replace it. Like a favorite toy or bed, a scratching surface is usually best loved when it has been broken in properly. What looks ragged to you may feel comfortable to your pet. More importantly, the post has the cat's scent all over it.

If you replace a familiar post with a new one, a cat might refuse to use the new item, sinking its claws into curtains or furniture instead.

The Beckoning Cat

Many legends and stories of cats survive in Japanese literature, the most enduring image being that of the Maneki-neko, the listening or beckoning cat. The beckoning cat acts as a charm to attract good fortune and as an amulet to ward off evil.

Japanese Cats

★ Pet cats were introduced into Japan from China in the reign of Emperor Ichijo, who ruled from 986 to 1011. It is recorded that on the tenth day of the fifth moon, the emperor's white cat gave birth to five white kittens, and a nurse was appointed to see that they were brought up as carefully as royal princes.

★ When Emperor Ichijo decided to forbid the use of cats as working animals, there were terrible repercussions for the silk industry. Without cats to keep them under control, mice began to eat all of the silkworm cocoons. The silk manufacturers placed statues of cats around the cocoons to scare the mice away, but to no avail. Eventually, the emperor was obliged to put the cats back to work to save the silk industry.

★ In Tokyo and Kyoto, there are still temples dedicated to cats. These are places of worship as well as necropoleis for cats. Outside, people hang prayer boards for cats that are sick or have gone missing.

A commemorative stamp of *Black Cat* by Japanese artist Hishida Shunso (1874–1911), who was known for his paintings of cats.

A fearsome cat statue standing guard outside a temple in Kyoto.

SOCIABLE BREEDS

- Abyssinian
- American Curl
- Balinese
- Birman
- Bombay
- British Shorthair
- Burmese
- Colorpoint Shorthair
- Egyptian Mau
- Havana Brown
- Himalayan
- Japanese Bobtail
- Javanese
- LaPerm
- Maine Coon
- Manx
- Norwegian Forest Cat
- Oriental Shorthair
- Persian
- Ragdoll
- Scottish Fold
- Siamese
- Siberian
- Singapura
- Snowshoe
- Somali
- Sphynx
- Tonkinese
- Turkish Angora
- Turkish Van

Hello Kitty balloon at Macy's Thanksgiving Day Parade in New York.

HELLO KITTY

Hello Kitty is a cat character designed by Yuko Shimizu for the Japanese company Sanrio, which specializes in *kawaii* (cute) products. A female Japanese Bobtail wearing a red bow, Hello Kitty first appeared in 1974 and has gone on to become a global phenomenon, adorning numerous consumer products, from purses to home appliances.

The Bobtail's short, stumpy tail is tightly curved and looks like a pompom.

Japanese Jewel

Japan's national cat is the Japanese Bobtail.

"In drawing my cats, I always commence by drawing the ears first; in every case I do this, and if I try any other way the proportions are certain to go wrong."
Louis Wain

The *Acrobats* by Louis Wain, who was famous for his illustrations of anthropomorphic cats.

The Art of Cat Fancy

🐾 A person who breeds or shows cats is called a cat fancier. Each country with an active band of cat fanciers has one or more governing bodies that keep a register of cats and their lineage, and set down rules and regulations for cat shows. The first ever cat registry, the National Cat Club (NCC), was established in England in 1887.

🐾 The founder and first president of the NCC was an artist named Harrison Weir. In 1889, he authored a book called *Our Cats and All About Them*. Weir is still referred to as the "father of the cat fancy."

🐾 Another artist succeeded Harrison as president of the NCC in 1890. Louis Wain was known for his whimsical cat illustrations that appeared in newspapers and on greeting cards and postcards.

CATGUT

✤ Despite the name, catgut has very little to do with cats. Catgut is a tough cord made from the intestines of certain animals—sheep, hogs, and horses—but not cats. It is used mainly for surgical sutures and the strings of musical instruments, tennis rackets, and archery bows.

✤ There are several theories about why the cord became known as catgut. A popular explanation is that, when the cords were first used for musical instruments centuries ago, the sound they produced was much like the sound that cats make when they are mating or being persecuted, as was common at the time.

✤ Today, with the advent of synthetic materials, there is little need for any animals' intestines to be used for such products.

A Cup of...

The Teacup Persian is bred to be small—only about 6 or 7 pounds (270 or 315 g) at adulthood.

Persians are generally placid and gentle by nature, and as kittens are playful and mischievous.

Trimming Your Cat's Claws

Active cats keep their claws trimmed through the wear and tear of everyday living, but if a cat is not scratching regularly and wearing down its claws, it is important to trim them. An indoor cat's claws may need regular clipping. Older cats that spend less time exercising and using a scratching post will also require more frequent trims.

✳ Claw clippers do not have to be made specifically for cats to be safe for your pet. If you have a set of trimmers made for dogs that are the right size for your feline, you can use them. Many cat owners also find that human fingernail clippers work well. What matters most is that you are comfortable using the trimmers you choose.

✳ To trim the claws, gently expose them. Each claw has a white tip and a pink quick. The pink quick is where the blood vessels are, and must not be clipped. Remove the white tip in a straight line. Cutting into the quick is painful and will cause bleeding. Applying a drop of mineral oil on the cat's claw can make it easier to see the quick.

✳ If you accidentally cut the quick when trimming a cat's claws, apply some styptic powder to the area to stop the bleeding. This practical product speeds the clotting process. If you do not have any styptic powder—or cannot find it in the midst of an emergency—you can substitute several household products. A little cornstarch, a wet tea bag, or a bar of soap will also help to stop bleeding. If you cannot get the wound to clot, contact a veterinarian promptly.

Claw clippers

If you are in doubt about how to trim your cat's claws properly, ask a veterinarian to show you.

NAPTIME TRIMS

One of the easiest ways to trim a cat's claws is to perform the task while your pet is sleeping. You might be able to cut all of the claws or just a few at a time this way, but whatever the case it will be a less stressful event for your feline friend. If the cat wakes up and resists, put the clippers away. You will have another trimming opportunity as soon as the cat naps again, which is sure to be soon.

MIRACULOUS SURVIVAL SKILLS

A massive earthquake hit Taiwan in 1999, killing more than 2,400 people. Eighty days later, a cat was found in a collapsed building in Chaitung—alive. Although injured, she recovered completely.

DEM BONES

A cat has 230 bones in its body. Of these, 10 percent are in its tail.

MOTION SICKNESS

If your cat experiences motion sickness when riding in an automobile or on an airplane, ask a veterinarian about the possibility of using a tranquilizer for long trips. Natural remedies are also available to prevent this common problem.

Why Do Cats Like to Perch in High Places?

Most cats feel safest when they are perched on something high. Their risk of being attacked from above is far greater when they are on the ground or floor. This risk is significantly lowered when cats are elevated. The feeling of security is one of the reasons that many cats like to climb onto tall furniture. If you have a dog, it may be a good idea to buy or build a carpeted tower for the cat, so that it can escape to higher ground whenever it feels the need. Some cats even like to eat on elevated surfaces. Cats also view height as a sign of status. The cat at the top of the cat tree is usually the "top cat" indeed.

A mother cat searching for prey in order to teach hunting techniques to her kittens.

LOOK WHAT I BROUGHT YOU!

Many free-roaming cats will bring prey home to their owners occasionally.

☆ Some owners interpret this behavior as a cat's way of showing off its kill and seeking praise. More likely, however, the cat is treating its owner like family—feline family, that is. Upon bringing home prey, a cat typically calls its owner by meowing loudly, in the same way as a mother cat when she brings home prey for her kittens.

☆ If you are bothered by this act, as many owners are, try not to show it. The cat is telling you that it cares about you. If you admonish your pet or scream, the cat may take this response as a rejection. Instead, do your best to remain calm. If possible, dispose of the prey. If the cat will not let you, offer it a toy or treat as a distraction to avert its attention.

On the Prowl

✳ If your cat is a hunter, you may notice that it wants to be outside the most around dawn and dusk. This is when small mammals, a cat's preferred prey, are most active. If you want to discourage the cat from hunting, keep it indoors during these peak times.

✳ Don't be surprised if the cat comes home with a bird now and then. Some cats possess intense hunting urges. Unlike rodents, birds are active during the day, and a deeply ingrained hunting instinct will lead a cat to settle for this slightly less coveted choice of quarry.

✳ You can discourage a cat from hunting by feeding it regularly—hungry cats tend to hunt more often. However, hunting is a deeply ingrained activity for many cats, whether it is necessary for their survival or not. A hungry cat will use hunting to supplement its diet; a well-fed cat will capture and then play with its prey.

✳ Mother cats catch prey purely as a means of teaching their kittens how to hunt, pouncing on the victim over and over to show her offspring how it is done. Toys that simulate this act of catching prey may be helpful in reducing your cat's hunting urges.

Try feeding your cat tougher chunks of meat, so that it feels it is wrestling with a huge wildebeest.

An Oriental Shorthair out on the prowl. The bell on its collar may help to alert potential prey.

BELLING THE CAT

The only sure way to stop a cat from hunting is to keep the cat indoors, but attaching a bell to its collar can help to alert birds and rodents to the presence of a feline predator. Collars are also available with sonic units for the same purpose.

TALK ABOUT VARIETY

Oriental Shorthairs are often called Ornamentals, because they come in more than 300 different color patterns.

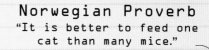

Norwegian Proverb

"It is better to feed one cat than many mice."

ARE YOU SUPERSTITIOUS?

✤ A black cat entering your house is said to be good luck, but if you chase it out of your home, it will take all of your good fortune with it.

✤ Some people say that it is a sign of good luck if a cat sneezes in the morning. A single sneeze at any time is thought to mean that rain is on the way.

✤ Be careful if you see a cat turn around three times, because some think it foretells an argument.

The shining jet black Bombay.

CHEERS FOR THE CHARTREUX!

Chartreux cats were named for the Carthusian monks who originally bred these cats for the purpose of ridding their monastery of mice. Legends state that the breed's ancestors were feral mountain cats from the area that is now Syria. It is said that returning crusaders brought the cats home with them to Grenoble, France, during the 13th century. Some say that the monks rewarded the cats for their work by allowing them to sample the Chartreuse liqueur that the order was famous for making.

Chartreux cat

Carthusian monk

SHORTHAIRED BREEDS

- Abyssinian
- American Curl
- American Shorthair
- American Wirehair
- Bengal
- Bombay
- British Shorthair
- Burmese
- Chartreux
- Colorpoint Shorthair
- Cornish Rex
- Devon Rex
- Egyptian Mau
- Exotic Shorthair
- Japanese Bobtail
- Korat
- Manx
- Ocicat
- Oriental Shorthair
- Scottish Fold
- Selkirk Rex
- Siamese
- Singapura
- Snowshoe
- Sphynx
- Tonkinese

A Growing Problem

Veterinarians see cats with life-threatening illnesses every day, but which illness is the biggest threat to your pet? Diabetes? Cancer? Heart disease? The answer is obesity. This dangerous condition is among the most common causes of all three of these serious illnesses, as well as many others.

★ Pet obesity is a growing problem throughout the world. In the United States, a 2011 study by the Association for Pet Obesity Prevention (APOP) found over 53 percent of cats to be overweight or obese.

★ An average cat should weigh about 7–11 pounds (3–5 kg). Obviously, this will vary with different breeds, so check with a veterinarian about what is right for your cat.

★ There are several medical reasons why a cat may be overweight, so take your pet to the veterinarian for a thorough checkup before embarking on a diet. If the vet recommends a weight-loss plan, follow it carefully—be aware that food formulas can differ dramatically in calorie density, so always check labels carefully. The vet may also advise more exercise, so make some time to play with the cat every day.

IS YOUR CAT FAT?

❶ *Does the cat's belly protrude?* *A pot belly, sometimes called an apron, is one of the most obvious signs of obesity in cats.*

❷ *Can you feel the cat's hips and ribs easily?* *Neither should be prominent. If you have to push to find these bones, however, the cat is likely overweight.*

❸ *Does the cat have an hourglass figure?* *Look at your standing pet from above. There should be an inward curve between its hips and ribs. If this curve is absent—or if it curves outward instead—the cat needs to lose some weight.*

❹ *What does the scale say?* *Weighing a cat regularly is the easiest ways to make sure that your pet stays at a healthy weight.*

WAKE-UP CALL
Chubby cats sleep longer than skinny ones. As heavier cats lose weight, they spend less time sleeping.

In 1504, Albrecht Dürer produced an engraving of the Garden of Eden that featured a cat sitting at the foot of the tree of life, its tail curled around Eve's legs.

Cats in Art

✳ After faring rather badly in religious art in medieval times, the situation for cats in art began to improve during the Renaissance period (around 14th–17th centuries). The great Renaissance artist Leonardo da Vinci was fascinated by cats, and drew many studies of them in various poses.

✳ By the 17th century, some painters had begun to include a cat in portraits; the cat usually looked extremely relaxed and was often sitting beside a fire.

✳ By the 18th century, cats had become a regular feature in all forms of art. Swiss artist Gottfried Mind (1768–1814) concentrated on cats almost exclusively as subjects for his work, and became known as the "Raphael of cats."

✳ During the 19th century, cats were a popular theme with French artists, especially Théophile Steinlen, who drew thousands of cats. Edouard Manet also painted many cats. He, James Tissot, and Eugène Delacroix contributed portrayals of cats to the book *Les Chats* by Champfleury, one of the earliest scholarly books about cats, first published in 1868.

✳ Cats have long been popular subjects for art in the East as well as the West, especially in Japan—in the 19th century, for example, Utagawa Kuniyoshi produced many beautiful paintings of cats.

FAMOUS PAINTINGS OF CATS

✦ *Still Life with Cat and Fish* (1728) by Jean-Baptiste-Siméon Chardin

✦ *Cat Fight* (1786–88) by Goya

✦ *Woman With a Cat* (1875) by Pierre-Auguste Renoir

✦ *Still-life With Cat* (1899) by Paul Gauguin

✦ *Children Playing with a Cat* (1908) by Mary Cassatt

✦ *Wounded Bird and Cat* (1938) by Pablo Picasso

A cat in a naturalistic pose is a prominent feature in *The Merchant's Wife* (1918) by Russian artist Boris Kustodiev.

HOME SWEET (NEW) HOME

It is truly amazing how outdoor cats always seem to find their way home, but what happens if you move? Will your pet adjust and remember where its new home is located? Chances are good that the cat will acclimate just fine, provided that you take a few precautions.

★ Unpack all of the cat's belongings as soon as possible. Having its regular food and dishes, bed, and even its toys will help your pet understand that this new place is now home.

★ Try to get at least one room settled for the cat right away, and keep your pet there while you organize the rest of the new residence. After a day or two, increase the cat's access to other areas of the home. Your pet will need at least a week or two of indoor time (and access to a litter box) before you can move on to venturing outdoors. It can take up to six months for a cat to become fully adapted to its new home and area.

★ During this acclimation period, you may find that the cat adjusts surprisingly well to indoor life. If so, you may wish to consider keeping your feline friend inside for good, away from outdoor dangers. If not, make sure that you do not open the door too soon or the cat may try to return to your previous address. Cats are known for traveling many miles to former homes.

★ Plan the cat's first outing close to a mealtime. Doing so will encourage your pet to come home sooner rather than later. Any cat that is allowed to roam freely outdoors should be sterilized, but this is especially important in the event of a move. A neutered cat will not only be accepted more easily by the neighborhood felines, but it will also be less prone to wandering behavior.

BUTTER FEET

You may have heard that putting butter on a cat's feet will prevent it from getting lost when it moves to a new home, but this old wives' tale does not work. Even the premise is sketchy. Some people think that the cat will lap the butter off its paws and simultaneously take in the scent of its new abode. Others insist that the cat is removing the scent of its old home. The truth is that cats dislike anything sticky on their paws.

Sleeping in its favorite bed with its favorite toy can help a cat to settle into its new home.

Unusual Ears

Most cats have upright, triangular shaped ears, but two notable variations have occurred through spontaneous mutation. The American Curl has ears that curl backward; the Scottish Fold has ears that fold forward.

AMERICAN CURL

The American Curl's distinguishing feature comes from its unique ear cartilage, which causes the ears to curl backward. The breed originated in Lakewood, California, in 1981. John and Grace Luga adopted two kittens whose ears curled back this way. When one of the kittens reached adulthood and produced a litter of her own, two of the offspring shared this characteristic. It was then determined that the trait could be passed from one generation to the next, paving the way for the development of the American Curl breed.

American Curl kittens are born with straight ears, which then curl and uncurl until remaining in their final position when the kitten is around four months old.

Scottish Fold

The Scottish Fold is so-named because of the way its ears fold forward. Cats are born with straight ears, but in most cases they start to fold around 3–4 weeks after birth. A shepherd named William Ross discovered this unusual breed on a farm in the Tayside region of Scotland in 1961.

As well as its distinctive folded ears, the Scottish Fold is also known for being especially fond of dogs.

> No, it would not be funny if you turned on the faucet.

A Persian taking refuge in a bathroom sink to cool down.

Too Much Sun

Excessive sun exposure can be just as dangerous for cats as it is to people. White-haired cats are the most susceptible, but any cat can suffer from sunburn or even skin cancer, particularly on its ears or nose. If your cat spends time outdoors, be sure to provide it with plenty of shady spots. Also, keep the cat inside when the sun is at its most brutal—typically between 11 A.M. and 1 P.M. Do not use sunscreen on a cat. Neither products made for people nor ones formulated for dogs are safe to use on cats.

Why Do Cats Sleep in Strange Places?

Cats like to sleep in unusual places and will choose from a wide range of localities.

✳ Cats enjoy curling up in confined spaces that make them feel protected and secure, and are particularly attracted by a soft, warm location such as a bed. A laundry basket is also very desirable to a cat. Warm clothes and linens from the dryer feel wonderful to a cat looking for a comfortable spot to take a nap.

✳ Conversely, don't be surprised if you find your cat sleeping in the bathroom sink. Many cats, especially longhaired breeds, enjoy curling up in an empty basin as a means of staying cool during warm weather. Some cats will even nap in the sink in the dead of winter. Curling up in this small round space that fits their bodies so well probably makes them feel safe.

No cat could resist the lure of a laundry basket full of warm clothes and linens.

MY, WHAT PRETTY TEETH YOU HAVE

Keeping a cat's teeth clean is an important part of maintaining your pet's good health.

1 Ease the cat into the idea of having its teeth brushed by getting it used to having your fingers in its mouth. To make the concept more appealing (or at least tolerable) for the cat, dip your fingers in some water from a can of drained tuna or some warm chicken broth first. This preliminary step will be most effective if you choose one of the cat's favorite foods.

2 Before you begin brushing, collect your supplies—a soft toothbrush and a tube of feline toothpaste. One of the best ways to make brushing a pleasant experience for the cat is by being as efficient as possible.

3 Apply a pea-sized amount of toothpaste to the brush. Holding the brush at a 45-degree angle, gently move it in a circular motion, starting at the gum line. Brush one tooth at a time.

4 If the cat resists having its teeth brushed, try using a piece of damp gauze instead of the brush. You can also make the task easier on your pet by dividing the task into two or three sessions. Always praise the cat for its compliance.

FELINE FLAVORS

Feline toothpaste comes in a variety of flavors. Two of the most popular choices are poultry and seafood, but remember that every cat has its own taste preferences. If a cat does not like chicken or turkey, it will be less than impressed with poultry-flavored toothpaste. Never use human toothpaste on a cat. Feline toothpaste is designed to be swallowed, but consuming even a small amount of human toothpaste can make your pet sick.

Let me get this straight. You want me to pull it, not ride in it. Are you serious?

Touché
"Cats are smarter than dogs. You can't get eight cats to pull a sled through snow." Jeff Valdez

Cats are most at risk from road accidents at night.

MAKE IT A GOOD NIGHT

Staying out all night can be dangerous for cats.

* In addition to the elements and predators, automobiles pose an even greater risk when it is dark outside. Cats can be blinded temporarily by approaching headlights, making it difficult for the animals to get out of the way of the vehicles. Moreover, even a cautious driver may not see a tiny cat in the road at night until it is too late.

* If you do not want to wait up for your pet every night, consider installing a cat door so that the cat can come back inside when it is ready. Even the most outdoorsy cats enjoy having a warm, safe place to sleep at night.

* Entice a free-roaming cat to come home by serving a small meal of wet food at the same time each evening. To make the meal as appetizing as possible, pop the dish in the microwave for a few seconds before serving. The cat will soon make a point of coming home to eat this tasty hot meal and sleep in its nice, warm bed every night.

SELECTING A CAT DOOR

❖ A cat door, or cat flap, should be the right size for the cat. Most flaps measure about 7½ x 9½ inches (19 x 24 cm). If the cat weighs more than 18 pounds (800 g), look for an extra-large model to prevent your pet from getting stuck.

❖ If the cat is new to using a door of its own, buy a transparent door. Your pet will be less intimidated by walking through a flap if it can see what is on the other side.

❖ Some doors lock when not in use, so that owners can limit the time their pets spend outdoors. If you do not want the cat going outside at night, for example, simply lock the door at bedtime each night.

❖ Electronic doors come with a sensor that is placed on the cat's collar. These doors prevent other neighborhood cats or stray animals from entering your home.

❖ To prevent burglars from using the cat door, be sure to install it a reasonable distance from door handles and locks.

Who Should Go?

If you have children, you may wonder whether you should take them along when visiting a breeder.

- In most cases, the answer is yes. It is important to select the right animal for your family. Kids play a significant role in defining family dynamics, so you can see how different kittens react to younger family members. Assuming the visit goes well, meeting your children will also make the breeder more comfortable with the kitten's future home.

- Of course, you should check with the breeder first to make sure that it is okay for your kids to join you. Some breeders prefer to limit the number of people who visit their catteries for the simple reason that pregnant mothers and kittens are considerably more susceptible to diseases and infections.

- If the breeder would prefer only one or two visitors, involve your kids in the decision-making process by asking them what kind of kitten they want. Answers relating to looks are far less important than preferences in personality, but their opinions should definitely be heard and considered.

CHILD-FRIENDLY BREEDS

- American Bobtail
- American Curl
- American Shorthair
- Birman
- British Shorthair
- Burmese
- Cymric
- Egyptian Mau
- Exotic Shorthair
- Himalayan
- Japanese Bobtail
- Maine Coon
- Manx
- Norwegian Forest Cat
- Ocicat
- Persian
- Ragdoll
- Scottish fold
- Selkirk Rex
- Siberian
- Sphynx
- Tonkinese
- Turkish Van

If possible, take your children along when selecting a new pet so that you can see how both child and animal get along.

On Companionship
"What greater gift than the love of a cat?"
Charles Dickens

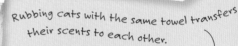

Rubbing cats with the same towel transfers their scents to each other.

FACE SHAPES

Face shapes fall into three basic categories:

✦ **Round:** Broad skull, small round-tipped ears, and a short broad nose. Breeds with round faces include the Persian and the Chartreux.

✦ **Intermediate:** Medium length, large pointed ears, and a slightly indented nose. Breeds with intermediate faces include the Maine Coon and the Abyssinian.

✦ **Wedge:** Triangular shaped, large pointed ears, and a long straight nose. Breeds with wedge-shaped faces include the Balinese and the Sphynx.

Round-faced cat!

"YOU SMELL FUNNY!"

In a multi-cat household, a trip to the veterinarian can affect the way feline friends interact with one another. When one cat visits the vet, it comes home with the scent of the hospital and anyone it encountered while there. The other cats are quick to pick up on these new odors and may treat their housemate like a complete stranger. To prevent negative interactions, use the same towel to rub each cat gently when you return from the appointment. Doing so will transfer their scents to one another and hopefully make the skeptics less suspicious of the strange new smells.

Ways to Entertain a Newly Indoor Cat

It is essential to provide indoor cats with physical and mental stimulation. Here are some ideas for how you can do this:

☆ **Invest in a scratching post.** A newly indoor pet is bound to feel a little frustrated—at least at first. You do not want it to release this aggravation by clawing at curtains or furniture.

☆ **Offer the cat a new toy each day.** You need not spend a lot of cash or get too fancy. Small, inexpensive playthings are often big hits, as are everyday objects like paper bags and cardboard boxes. The point is to keep the cat from feeling bored.

☆ **Buy toys that stimulate the hunting process.** If the cat was previously an avid hunter, having a quickly moving toy to pounce on will help ease your pet's predatory urges.

☆ **Place a bird feeder just outside the window.** Position the feeder in view of the window where the cat spends the most time. Sometimes just being able to see birds and other wildlife helps to ease a cat's frustration over not being outdoors.

☆ **Buy a window perch**. If none of the windows in your home has a wide enough sill for a cat to sit on, consider purchasing a window perch where the cat can sit or lie while looking out of the window.

☆ **Turn on the television.** Many cats enjoy watching other animals, whether in real life or on a TV screen. If your neighborhood is not full of birds or squirrels for the cat to watch out of the window, tune in to an animal TV channel or buy a wildlife video.

You do not need to spend lots of money on cat toys. Most cats love playing with cardboard boxes.

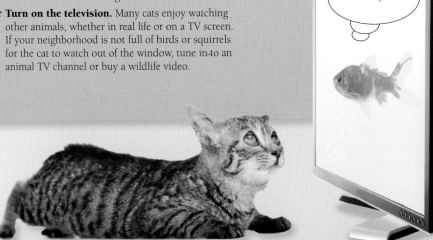

Cat's Cradle

The children's game cat's cradle has been played for centuries, but no one knows for certain where it began. Some people believe that the game originated in Asia and then spread throughout Europe and the rest of the world. All one needs to play the game is a loop of string, which is then looped around the hands and fingers and passed from one person to another through systematic twists and turns.

LIBRARY CATS

The use of cats as a form of rodent control in libraries dates back to ancient times. Cats living in the temples of ancient Egypt helped to protect the papyrus documents stored there; in medieval times, monks used cats to protect the precious manuscripts in their monasteries. The Russian Hermitage museum and library in St. Petersburg has famously been home to hundreds of cats over the centuries. In 1987, the Library Cat Society (LCS) was formed in the United States to promote the establishment of cats in libraries. Today, the tradition of library cats is as strong as ever, with hundreds living in libraries around the world, acting both as rodent controllers and as mascots.

UNDEMANDING BREEDS

- Birman
- Bombay
- Chartreux
- Havana Brown
- Himalayan
- Nebelung
- Persian
- Ragdoll
- Russian Blue
- Scottish Fold
- Selkirk Rex

I Shall Call You...

The Selkirk Rex is the only cat breed that was named after an actual person. The breed was developed by Jeri Newman of Montana, who named it after her stepfather.

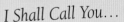

Ahem! I wouldn't mind a little privacy, you know.

THINGS THAT GO FLUSH IN THE NIGHT

Some owners have taught their cats how to use a toilet instead of a litter box. Cats are remarkably intelligent animals that can easily learn how to utilize this human bathroom fixture. Do bear in mind, though, that you will need to leave the lid up at all times for a toilet-trained pet. You can also teach a cat to flush when it has finished. Don't be surprised if the water bill increases, however, because some cats get quite a thrill out of this step, repeating it over and over whether necessary or not.

GOING VIRAL

In 2007, a video of a cat named Gizmo flushing a toilet over and over—and over—spread like wildfire across the internet. The story that accompanied the video in the popular forwarded email message stated that the cat's owners, Jim and Jennifer, could not figure out why their water bill was so expensive all of a sudden—until one day they discovered the clever little water waster in action. According to www.snopes.com, the video is legitimate, but the story is erroneous. The cat's actual owners, Nick and Scarlet of Santa Clara, California, say that they discovered their kitten's hidden talent one afternoon when Scarlet was home alone and heard the toilet flush. Gizmo was still flushing away when Nick arrived home, so he grabbed his video camera. The rest is internet history.

KEEPING FIDO OUT

No one likes to talk about it, but it is one of the most common problems that multi-species households face. If you own both a cat and a dog, you must have a strategy for keeping pooch from snacking on the contents of kitty's litter box. Here are a few tried and true strategies:

✣ Remove waste from the litter box as soon as the cat uses it.

✣ Use a litter box with a cover and flap.

✣ Place a gate in the doorway to the room where you keep the box.

✣ Install a cat flap in the door to the room where the box is kept.

✣ Invest in an automatic litter box that removes waste from the box after the cat exits.

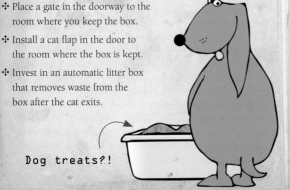

`Dog treats?!`

King of the Jungle

♣ The lion is the only true social cat, living in
groups called prides, in which lionesses hunt
together to achieve a kill. The size of a pride
is influenced by the availability of prey;
where hunting is good, prides are larger.

♣ The development of the lion's mane is under
the control of the male sex hormones. Neutering
a male lion, even after puberty, will cause
the mane to recede and even disappear.

SHAVE AND A HAIRCUT

Some owners of longhaired breeds
schedule regular appointments for
their cats with professional groomers.
Typically done seasonally, this spa day
for your pet may include a thorough
brushing to remove any mats, a bath,
and claw trimming. You may elect to
have the cat shaved down to avoid
mats from forming in the first place.
Many owners select a lion cut, which
involves shaving everything except the
ruff (around the neck) and the lower
sections of the legs and tail.

Spot the difference—a
Persian cat with a lion cut.

HANDLING A CAT

Never grab a cat by the scruff of its neck. Although kittens go limp when their mothers pick them up and carry them around this way, they do not react in the same way when a person uses this approach. Instead, place one hand under the cat's chest and use the other hand to support its rump. The safer the cat feels when it is with you, the more comfortable and relaxed it will be.

Mother cats only pick up their kittens by the scruff when they are tiny and weigh very little.

Feral cats sometimes live together in a colony and share available food.

Stray or Feral?

Question: What is the difference between a stray cat and a feral cat?

Answer: A stray cat is an animal that once had a home. It may be lost, or it may have been abandoned, but it is usually tame. A feral cat is a cat that was born to either a stray or another feral cat. Most feral cats do not know how to act around people because they have never been part of a human family. Many people think that feral cats cannot adapt to life in a home. The truth is that rescuing a feral cat can be a challenge to even the most experienced cat owner, but it is not an impossible task. Kittens are typically the easiest to tame, but each situation is different. If you are considering taking in a feral cat, talk to a veterinarian or the staff at a local shelter. They can answer any questions that you may have before you make a decision.

Fights Over Food

In general, cats are much less food aggressive than dogs, but when two or more cats share a home, dinnertime squabbles may arise. It is best to solve the problem before it snowballs into a bigger one. If left to fester, aggression issues can result in spraying as a means of marking territory, and even trips to the veterinary emergency room.

☆ Begin feeding the fighting cats on opposite sides of the room.

☆ Supervise meal times to make sure that every cat is able to eat its own food.

☆ If you schedule the cats' meals, be sure to stick to the schedule. Hungry cats are more likely to pick fights over food.

☆ Instead of schedule feeding, consider changing to a free-feeding routine. As long as none of the cats is overweight, free feeding can be a great way to discourage food aggression. Animals are less likely to fight over food when it is plentiful. Even if the dominant cat still wants to guard all the food, it cannot be in more than one place at a time, so make sure that you have at least as many dishes as cats.

☆ When the cats start to tolerate each other well at dinnertime, offer them a quick cat treat afterward. This edible reward will encourage continued affable behavior.

☆ **Note:** If the aggression over food is between a cat and a dog, the easiest solution is to raise the cat's dishes to where the dog cannot reach them—and keep the cat away from the dog when it is eating, of course.

BREAK IT UP—SAFELY

If you need to break up a fight between cats, don't get in the middle of the scuffle. To avoid getting scratched, use a broom with a long handle to separate the animals instead.

Freya

Freya was the Norse equivalent of Bastet, the Egyptian cat goddess of love and fertility. Freya traveled in a chariot that was pulled by large cats, originally portrayed as lynx but later as very large domestic cats. For a long time, people in Scandinavia used to put saucers of milk outside the door at night for Freya's cats.

Freya in her chariot pulled by cats.

Girls, Girls, Girls

If you want a purebred kitten, finding a female may be a bit of a challenge. Many breeders prefer to keep their female offspring so that these cats can be part of their breeding program in the future.

BIRTH CONTROL FOR YOUR CAT

✦ If you plan to breed a female cat but are not ready to do so just yet, you must be very careful when she comes into heat. Male cats will seek her out at every opportunity during this part of her cycle.

✦ You may want to talk to a veterinarian about putting a female cat on the pill until you are ready to breed her. Similar to the human birth control pill, the feline pill uses a reproductive hormone called progestin to prevent ovulation. Unlike the human medication, the feline form only needs to be given once a week. An even longer-acting injection is also available.

✦ Hormonal birth control carries certain risks, including uterine infections. These risks are higher when the medication is used for extended time periods. Once you are done breeding the cat, the best way to prevent future pregnancies is to have your pet spayed.

Vital Signs

★ **Temperature:** Normal feline body temperature is between 100 and 102°F (38 and 39°C).

★ **Pulse:** A healthy cat's heart beats between 110 and 160 times per minute. A younger cat will have a faster heartbeat, or pulse, than an older cat.

★ **Respiration:** Most cats take between 20 and 30 breaths per minute. This breathing rate is called respiration.

Two kittens are likely to bond more quickly and easily than two adult cats.

BETTER IN PAIRS

If your plan is to get two cats, it is better to acquire them together as kittens than to start with one and add the second one later. Kittens are far less territorial than adult cats, and two really are not any more trouble than one. If possible, select two littermates, because they will be bonded to each other already.

Can I come and join your family please?

SUSPICIOUS MINDS

Adult cats tend to be a bit hesitant to welcome newcomers to their household, and often accept a kitten more readily than a fellow adult cat.

Reasons to Adopt an Adult Cat

❋ Adult cats have established temperaments. A kitten's personality can change as it matures, but an adult has already developed its character traits.

❋ They have usually been socialized to people and other animals.

❋ They are almost always trained to use a litter box already. Although kittens learn quickly, adults typically arrive fully trained.

❋ Adult cats are usually better choices for families with young children. Kittens are far more vulnerable to accidental injuries than older cats.

❋ Adults are far less demanding than kittens. They require less exercise and playtime than their younger counterparts.

❋ They are much less likely to be destructive. Kittens often require a fair amount of supervision so that they do not scratch curtains and carpeting.

❋ Adult cats have usually been sterilized already.

❋ Adult cats need homes even more desperately than younger cats do. When shelters become inundated with kittens, older cats may be euthanized to make room for young animals that have a better chance at finding new homes. By adopting an adult cat, you just may be saving its life.

An adult cat is usually calmer and less demanding than a kitten.

YOUNG ADULTS FROM BREEDERS

Kittens that do not match the breed standard are usually easy to pick out relatively quickly, but it can take much longer to identify the kittens that will make good show cats. A kitten's coat and eye coloration can change a lot in its first year or two of life. Some breeders offer their young adult cats that did not reach show potential at a reduced price. Typically, these cats are still very young—barely more than kittens really. They can make excellent pets, especially for people who prefer a cat that is fully litter box trained and past the more demanding stages of kittenhood.

Pick me!

PET STORES ARE FOR SUPPLIES

More often than not, the kittens sold by pet stores are from kitten mills—large-scale commercial breeders that produce animals purely for profit. The best resource for buying a healthy, well-adjusted pet is a reputable breeder.

IF YOUR CAT DISLIKES AN IMPORTANT PERSON

If your cat is not wild about meeting new people, introducing your pet to someone who means a lot to you can be stressful for everyone involved. The meeting can be particularly frustrating if the cat takes an instant dislike to the new person. If this is a new roommate, spouse, or someone who will be spending a considerable amount of time with the cat, you need to solve the problem as soon as possible.

☆ One of the best ways to help the cat warm up to a new household member is to place this person in charge of your pet's care, at least for a while. In the beginning, you must refrain from caring for the cat completely. Ask the new household member to take care of everything from feeding the cat to giving it attention. This approach can be difficult for owners who are bonded closely with their pets, but it is often the most effective solution to this common problem.

☆ Set the new caregiver up for success by giving him or her access to all of the cat's favorite things—a toy, catnip, and of course edible treats. Long-term overindulgence with food can lead to obesity, but let the new person spoil the cat for now. You can wean your pet off the excess calories once the two of them have established a good relationship.

☆ If the cat still refuses to accept the new household member, don't give up. Stick with the plan just a bit longer. Instruct the new person to ignore any aggressive behavior from the cat. He or she should not allow the animal to bite or scratch, but punishing it in any way will only have a negative impact on the new relationship. Instead, the new person should take advantage of times when the cat acts friendly or tolerant. Rewards for positive behavior can range from a tasty treat to a belly scratch, if accepted. The cat just may discover that your new significant other is a fun addition to its home.

The more the cat has to rely on the new household member, the more quickly it will see that this person's presence is not a threat to its well-being.

The Devon Rex would look unusual even without its wavy coat, having a quizzical, pixie-like expression and huge, bat-like ears.

Happy Accidents

Sometimes a new cat breed appears when two cats mate and produce a kitten that looks completely different from either of its parents. This natural occurrence is referred to as spontaneous mutation. A curly coated kitten was born in an otherwise normal litter at a farm in Cornwall, England, in 1950 with no human intervention whatsoever. Breeders used the kitten to develop the Cornish Rex breed. Ten years later, another curly coated kitten was discovered in the neighboring English county of Devon. The kitten was used to develop the Devon Rex breed. Despite being geographical neighbors and both having curly coats, tests showed that the curls were caused by different genes, and so the Cornish Rex and the Devon Rex are two quite distinct breeds. Although it is not common, spontaneous mutation is not rare either.

The Cornish Rex was named after its place of origin and the Rex rabbit, which has very soft, velvety fur.

TO MATCH THEIR COATS, OF COURSE
The Cornish Rex and the Devon Rex not only have curly coats, but they also have curled whiskers.

ODD-LOOKING BREEDS

* Cornish Rex
* Devon Rex
* Manx
* Minskin
* Munchkin
* Scottish Fold

Bufo
marinus

RARE BREEDS
• American Wirehair
• Burmilla
• California Spangled
• Cheetoh
• Elf Cat
• German Rex
• Highlander
• Kinkalow
• Lambkin Dwarf Cat
• Minskin
• Munchkin
• Ojos Azules
• Peke Face
• Serengeti
• Sokoke
• Toyger

Toxic Toads

✦ Toads emit a foul-tasting substance. Cats that have come into contact with a toad often shake their head vigorously in an effort to get rid of the horribly bitter taste. They may salivate excessively and even vomit.

✦ In warmer parts of the world, there are species of toad that emit a substance that is poisonous to cats. In the United States and Australia, for example, one of the most common poisonous varieties is *Bufo marinus* (known as the giant toad, marine toad, or cane toad).

✦ Cats that have caught a poisonous toad species may have difficulty breathing or even seize. Flush the cat's mouth with water to remove as much of the toxic substance as possible—a garden hose often works well for this purpose. Seek veterinary treatment immediately. Even if you only suspect that the cat has been poisoned by a toad, a vet visit is still a smart idea.

The short-legged Munchkin is named after the little people in *The Wizard of Oz*.

THE HISTORY OF CAT LITTER

For many years, people used sand or dirt to fill the boxes where their cats eliminated. Although these materials were literally dirt cheap, they were also messy and did nothing to diminish unpleasant smells. So who came up with the great invention of cat litter?

❀ In the 1930s, New York entrepreneur George Plitt made a business of selling ashes from burned wood to cat owners as an alternative to dirt; he named his product Kleen Kitty. However, although ashes were better at controlling odor, they also made a mess when tracked by the animals.

❀ In 1947, Edward Lowe of Minnesota decided to package absorbent clay and sell it as cat box filler. Lowe visited cat shows where he could demonstrate and promote his new product, which he named Kitty Litter. He later experimented with various ingredients that made his groundbreaking product even more efficient. In 1964, Lowe created the Tidy Cat brand of cat litter.

❀ Innovations to the cat litter industry continued. In 1984, a Houston biochemist named Thomas Nelson invented the first clumping cat litter.

❀ Today, owners can choose between clay, clumping, and even gel-based cat litter. If you do not mind shelling out the extra cash, you can even buy an automatic litter box that cleans itself.

TYPES OF
CAT LITTER
• Clay
• Clumping/scoopable
• Corn
• Flushable
• Newspaper
• Paper or wood pellets
• Reusable
• Sand-based
• Scented
• Silica crystals
• Wheat husk

Silica crystals are the most absorbent type of cat litter.

Sailors and Cats

A ship's cat was believed to bring good luck, as well as helping to keep the ship free from rodents. In some places, the wives of fishermen used to keep a black cat in their homes until the boats returned. It was believed that if the cat escaped or was lost, the outcome could be fatal for the men.

THE ARISTOCATS (from left): Edgar, the scheming butler; Thomas O'Malley, the street-smart alley cat; Duchess, the aristocratic heiress; Duchess's three kittens—Toulouse (orange); Marie (white); and Berlioz (gray).

Famous Feline Movies

Cats have played starring or key roles in a number of feature-length movies, both animated and live action. Here are a few of them:

★ **Bell, Book and Candle:** In this 1958 movie, a feline character named Pyewacket does a little matchmaking for his owner, a witch played by Kim Novak. The movie helped to inspire the popular television series *Bewitched*, which launched in 1964. In the movie, Pyewacket was portrayed by a Siamese cat, the first of its breed to be in a film.

★ **The Incredible Journey:** Disney's 1963 movie is about two dogs and a cat (a male Siamese named Tao) that get lost while their owners are on vacation and have to make their way home through the Canadian wilderness. Disney recast Tao as a female Himalayan named Sassy in the 1993 remake *Homeward Bound: The Incredible Journey*.

★ **That Darn Cat:** In 1965, Hayley Mills starred in Disney's movie about a cat that ends up saving the life of a kidnapped bank teller. In 1997, Disney remade the film with Christina Ricci in the Hayley Mills role. The cat, D.C. ("Darn Cat"), was played by a Siamese in the original, and by a Maine Coon in the remake. The movies were based on the 1963 novel *Undercover Cat* by the Gordons, a husband and wife crime writing duo.

★ **The Aristocats:** This 1970 animated Disney movie tells the story of a cat named Duchess, voiced by Eva Gabor, and her three kittens. When their owner passes away, the cats inherit everything—the house, the money, and the resentful butler who schemes to get rid of the feline family so that the fortune will become his own. Fortunately, a street-smart alley cat named Thomas O'Malley comes to the rescue.

★ **Cats & Dogs:** In this 2001 movie, an evil white Persian named Mr. Tinkles attempts to make all humans allergic to dogs so that cats can rule the world. The 2010 follow-up, *Cats & Dogs 2: The Revenge of Kitty Galore*, sees cats and dogs joining forces against Kitty, a hairless cat who is seeking world domination in revenge for the ridicule and rejection she suffered after losing all her fur during a mission against dogs.

Award Winners

The PATSY (Picture Animal Top Star of the Year) was like the Academy Award of the animal kingdom until it was discontinued in 1986. Feline winners included:

❖ **Orangey** (1952 & 1962): The orange tabby star of the movies Rhubarb and Breakfast at Tiffany's. Orangey was the only two-time winner of the award.

❖ **Pyewacket** (1959): The Siamese cat in Bell, Book and Candle.

❖ **Syn** (1966): The Siamese cat in That Darn Cat!

❖ **Morris** (1973): The tabby spokescat for 9Lives cat food, for his work in the commercials.

The cat famously stroked by Blofeld, the arch villain in several James Bond movies, was a chinchilla Persian.

Index

Dedication
For Autumn.

Picture Credits
AGIP / Rue des Archives / Mary Evans Picture Library page 2; Everett Collection / Rex Features page 59; NASA / J.P. Harrington (U. Maryland) and K.J. Borkowski (NCSU) page 64 (below left); 20th Century Fox / Everett Collection / Rex Features page 86; The Art Archive / Musée du Louvre Paris / Gianni Dagli Orti page 107; Mary Evans Picture Library page 149; Stapleton Collection / Corbis page 154; Francis G. Mayer / Corbis page 163; Snap / Rex Features page 184.

While every effort has been made to credit contributors, Quarto would like to apologize should there have been any omissions or errors—and would be pleased to make the appropriate correction for future editions of the book.